W9-DAY-196

THE SEXUAL LIFE

A SCIENTIFIC TREATISE DESIGNED

For Advanced Students and the Professions

EMBRACING

THE NATURAL SEXUAL IMPULSE, NORMAL SEXUAL HABITS AND PROPAGATION, TOGETHER WITH SEXUAL PHYSIOLOGY AND HYGIENE

BY

C. W. MALCHOW, M.D.

PROFESSOR OF PROCTOLOGY AND ASSOCIATE IN CLINICAL MEDICINE, HAMLINE UNIVERSITY COLLEGE OF PHYSICIANS AND SURGEONS; PRESIDENT OF PHYSICIANS' AND SURGEONS' CLUB; MEMBER HENNEPIN COUNTY MEDICAL SOCIETY, MINNESOTA STATE MEDICAL SOCIETY, AMERICAN MEDICAL ASSOCIATION, ETC., ETC.

FIFTH EDITION

ST. LOUIS
C. V. MOSBY COMPANY
1917

TO MY MOTHER

MARIE GERICKE-MALCHOW

To whom I owe most for whatever I may be; whose physical deformity inspires gentleness, and whose simple, true life will ever command my highest esteem

THIS VOLUME IS MOST REVERENTIALLY DEDICATED BY

THE AUTHOR

PREFACE

The physician sees many things that are not ordinarily exposed to view. He is called upon for advice and information upon matters that are held secret and sacred. His work often soils his hands with unnameable filth and jeopardizes his comfort and safety; yet when pursued in the spirit of philanthropy and scientific endeavor, its repulsive features serve but to bring out in bold relief the ennobling virtues.

Sex is the central fact of life, and owing to the urgent necessity for enlightenment upon a subject that greatly affects, directly or indirectly, every member of society, prudery and mawkish modesty should be disregarded. When others do not intelligently discuss delicate matters regarded as peculiarly intimate, personal and shameful, it becomes a part of the physician's duty so to do.

The situations created by an improper exercise of the sexual function in marriage are many and complicated, and the problems presented are delicate and perplexing. In dealing with these situations there is required not only a thorough knowledge of this function in all its relations, but also tact, sagacity, and a knowledge of human nature, which are not usually taught in the curriculum of our colleges.

Civilization is as yet but a mere film of refinement and intelligence lightly placed upon a foundation of ignorance and superstition. Every physician must at the present time be a missionary and in his work of pointing out the way to health, (without which there can be no happiness) he must expect to receive, oftentimes, the treatment accorded his theological fellow at the hands of barbarity.

The people look to the medical profession for the restoration and preservation of health, and modern medical science is directed toward the prevention of disease. The office of the physician is not only that of a healer, but that of a sanitarian also, and the latter becomes the higher office from the fact that the interests of the many are superior to those of the individual.

In the present age it is not so much what a practitioner of medicine is able to cure as what he is able to prevent that marks him as a benefactor. After all, the prime object of the physician's existence is to keep his patients in health; when disease overtakes them it is his business to restore them to health as speedily as possible.

When a patient seeks the aid of his physician, the latter, in addition to prescribing for him, gives him certain advice and suggestions as to his mode of life, which will aid materially in his restoration to health. If the patient is sensible and possessed of good judgment, he will continue to live in the manner prescribed, and in the majority of cases avoiding a recurrence of the original trouble. If the physician could have given his advice before the appearance of the ailment, and the patient had followed it, the chances are strongly in favor of the supposition that the trouble would never have appeared. In multiplying this condition and extending it to a community instead of a patient, a large amount of illness will have been prevented.

In preventing unhappiness and disease in marriage, a heavy responsibility is imposed upon the physician because of the number and importance of the interests involved.

In his capacity as the guardian of his patient's health, the physician will not have done his whole duty unless he gives such instruction and information as will be conducive to sexual health and happiness, and point out what leads to disease and misery.

There is comparatively little authentic literature upon sexual physiology and many members of the profession do not to-day fully appreciate its significance. Very much nonsense is written, and upon investigation it will be found that the average library contains many books that are calculated to arouse and appeal to the passions, but very little is to be found that is really instructive or acts as food for thought upon the topic that greatly affects all classes and kinds of people. An effort has been made to present herewith something solid and to give only scientific and established facts—such as will better enable those who are interested and consulted upon these matters to obtain and impart rational information.

The duty of reforming the morals of the community is not within the province of the physician, and though individual reformation may be accomplished through his agency by giving instruction in matters relating to sexual hygiene and the ailments of sexual life, yet this phase of the question has largely been left with those to whom it rightfully belongs.

To seek out and present the most vital facts of life is fraught with many difficulties, and the kindly encouragement given me by many members of the clergy and the legal, as well as the medical, profession has been a great aid in my labors. Such authorities as I have had access to have been freely consulted, and the works of Havelock Ellis, Krafft-Ebing, and others, have been made use of, for which I desire to make due acknowledgement.

In the previous edition of this book a number of quotations were employed to illustrate some of the points brought out, but inasmuch as they neither add to nor dertract from the work, it has been deemed advisable to omit them.

CONTENTS.

CHAPTER I.

SEXUAL SENSE.

CHAPTER II.

SEXUAL PASSION

CHAPTER III.

FEMALE SEXUAL SENSE

CHAPTER IV.

MALE SEXUAL SENSE.

CHAPTER V

THE COPULATIVE FUNCTION

CHAPTER VI

THE ACT OF COPULATION

CHAPTER VII

SEXUAL HABITS IN THE MARRIED

CHAPTER VIII

HYGIENIC SEXUAL RELATIONS

CHAPTER IX.

SEXUAL INEQUALITY

CHAPTER X

COPULATION AND PROPAGATION

CHAPTER XI.

NERVOUS WOMEN

INTRODUCTION.

Man is naturally a social being, and the sum total of all that goes to make life worth living may be expressed by the word "contentment." The pursuit of happiness is the aim of all human endeavor, and there is nothing that contributes so largely to the happiness of adult human life (when actual necessities are available) or causes the person more secret concern and anxiety, than his or her individual sexual relations. Society and civilization are founded and builded upon the home, and the home is not a mansion or a hovel, but is the result of the assumption of the sexual relation. If the home cannot or does not supply the sexual and most of the social needs of its founders, then it cannot be called home in the full sense of the word.

The physical, the mental, and the moral being is the result of heredity, environment, and education. Science does not take cognizance of sentiment, for that is the product of culture, and they who permit themselves to be governed by a sentimentality that ignores or conflicts with the established inexorable laws of nature, must inevitably meet with disaster.

We know nothing — absolutely nothing — except that which we have learned; and our knowledge consists of what we have acquired by personal experience, together with that which has been imparted to us by others. The beneficent author of our being intended that we should be social creatures, and receive the greatest and most important part of our knowledge by the information of others. The average person is accorded but very meager facilities for the acquisition of knowledge upon sexuality, and what little is obtained usually comes too late to be of practical value. Civilization, religion and social ethics forbid diversified sexual experience, and sternly decree that this must be strictly limited to the one with whom the marital relation has been assumed. Practically, and to the shame of society, be it said, this is applicable more especially to women; for knowledge of a single deviation from this prescribed edict insures social ostracism to the unfortunate woman to whom the finger of suspicion may be pointed, while these "indiscretions" on the part of the man are too frequently condoned. This injustice has not only created a double standard by which people are measured, but precludes the possibility of an unmarried woman obtaining the slightest personal knowledge of what is to become of the utmost importance to her.

Education by experience, which is the greatest and best of teachers, being denied her, and therefore out of the question, the only alternative remaining for the acquisition of information, is a reliance upon what is imparted to her. It is a deplorable fact that those who are best qualified to give this information are reluctant to impart it, owing to the delicacy of the subject, and the difficulty of presenting it in an acceptable manner. The mother of the girl, upon whom this duty naturally devolves, cannot bring herself to speak of it with any degree of intelligence, and even when attempts are made to convey ideas which must of necessity be the result of a decidedly limited personal experience that is most often very disappointing, not to say disagreeable, they are almost invariably improperly presented and falsely understood. Indeed, a large proportion of mothers pride themselves upon what they are pleased to term the "innocence" of their marriageable daughters and cherish the fond illusion that ignorance is always innocence, and want of knowledge the equivalent of virtue.

Very much time and energy is expended in teaching young people how to conduct themselves in society, how to make a good impression, and girls especially are educated in the art of being attractive and entertaining, and every effort is put forth in the endeavor to make a desirable matrimonial alliance, but no attention is given to what is all-important for the family welfare, for the young couples are left to themselves at the door of the bridal chamber with no rational education relative to their conduct within the confines of that sacred boudoir. Here, at the portal of life's crucial period, they are left to work out their own salvation, hampered, rather than assisted, by their previous training, with only a varying dream that has but a bare chance of being realized, but with never a word of proper instruction upon what is most vital for their future.

Most of the literature upon this topic does not seem to be forthcoming for the sole purpose of disseminating the exact truth and depicting the actual conditions, but it is the outgrowth of ulterior and mercenary motives, and, instead of being beneficial and wholesome, is too often the source of uncalled-for solicitude, apprehension and misery. The laity, as well as the profession, is with brazen affrontery repeatedly confronted with reading matter that is a veritable libel upon mankind, in which the usual physiological conditions are portrayed as being pathological states.

To counteract as far as possible, the baneful influences of current literature and to call attention to scientific truth, as well as to endeavor to throw a ray of light into what must be a deplorable obscurity, is the object of this publication.

CHAPTER I

SEXUAL SENSE

Definition of Sense—Self-Preservation and the Instinct for Propagation—Physical Causes of Pleasure and Pain—Three Cardinal Human Functions—Physical Wants and Mental Desires—The Greatest Longing of Adult Life is Sexual—Development of Special Senses—By the Faculty of Attention and the use of Memory, the Minds become Varied, According to Cerebral Impressions—The Ever-present Sexual Stimulus—Mental Effect of Physical Changes at Puberty—The Ruling Passion of Mature Life—Preferences are Varied and Sexuality is the Real Magnet that Attracts—Individual Love Born and Made Enduring by Association—Self-Confidence and Sexual Competence—Importance of Sexual Sense.

Sense may be said to be a perception or cognizance of an impression. When an impression arises spontaneously from the body it is known as instinct, and when it amounts to an urging from within we are in the habit of calling the feeling an impulse. When any given sensation is felt, all we can say with certainty is that there is an impression upon the sensorium in the brain. The cause may be some object of the external world, in which case the sensation will be objective; or the condition may be due to some excitement within the brain, in which instance the sensation is termed subjective. Judgments are often unconsciously based upon sensations.

The preservation of self is perhaps the strongest human instinct and is often alluded to as the "first law of nature." If we go but a step farther we find closely allied and intimately interwoven with this trait the desire to prolong or perpetuate self in the species, and with this basis we have the manifestation of sexuality, the sexual sense, or the instinct for propagation.

A state of health, ease or well-being is consistent only with a normal mind in a body where all of the organs perform their several functions harmoniously. It is more than probable that each cell in the body performs its function in unison with general consciousness. When this harmony or rythm becomes increased or exalted it is felt, and the consciousness of this sensation we call pleasure, because it is agreeable; but when this rythm is decreased and there is a lesser degree of unity, the lack of harmony occasions discomfort and we call this discord—pain.

It is necessary, then, for personal comfort, pleasure and happiness that we have, first, a physical condition in which there is a concordant cellular activity, which produces in each and every organ and tissue of the body an harmonious performance of its function; and, secondly, such an adjustment or relation with the external world which is in accord with our being and which permits the performance of our fundamental physical functions without offending ourselves or interfering with those with whom we come in contact.

The elementary conditions of the external world

are beyond our control, and hence we are compelled, for our safety, to adjust ourselves in harmonious relations thereto. If we do not hold ourselves in the proper relations toward gravity, heat, air, water, etc., we must invariably succumb, for it is necessary for our physical welfare that we conform to these natural laws.

Our mental state, however, is susceptible to other influences, and, being of a social nature, we are to a certain extent dependent upon one another, and are susceptible to and exert influences which affect our mental tranquillity. Amicable and desirable social relations partake of mutuality, and the more we have in common with each other, the more capable do we become for mutual helpfulness, while the degree of amicability is in direct ratio with the desire and the ability for gratification.

Nowhere do we find a better exemplification of this fact than in the sexual relation. If we have no wants or desires then there is no need of satiation or gratification. The degree of felicity is conditioned upon the intensity of the desire and the ability for its satisfaction. There is no greater pleasure or felicity conceivable than is occasioned by the satiation or gratification of the most intense desire. What, then, is the greatest desire of adult humanity?

During growth and before maturity there are two cardinal principles that actuate every living cell and every aggregation of cells, and these are—motion and nutrition. It would be impossible for the organism to obtain its required nutriment without motive power whereby it could appropriate to itself from its surroundings the wherewith to sustain and prolong or perpetuate its existence. After the cell or the organism has attained its maturity it becomes capable of not only prolonging its already existing physical state, but it acquires the faculty of giving off a part of itself for a separate existence, and the third fundamental function is added to the other two.

This third function is the inherent faculty of reproducing its kind, and thus we find that all living things possess a capacity for motion, nutrition and reproduction. All three are necessary for life, for without either, the kind would soon become extinct. Birth is the separation of offspring from parent, and living things owe their existence to a previous being.

These propensities are not confined to the individual cell but are possessed by every combination or aggregation of cells in separate and distinct organizations.

This applies to the human being as well as to all other living things, and though the function of reproduction is not absolutely essential to the mere existence of the individual body, yet in compliance with the laws of the indestructibility of matter and the preservation of self, this function becomes a part of the mature being, and inasmuch as it is not an absolute requisite for the maintenance of individual life, it becomes the first and, therefore, the greatest desire of the being.

In view of the above it would seem that though the reproductive function is not necessary for the temporary existence of the being, yet it is a part thereof and the very aim of its being, and therefore necessary to its natural life.

The fact that a complex organization, such as man, is in itself incapable of reproducing its kind, but is dependent upon a similar organic body for the fulfillment of this function, renders it a social creature, because it cannot by itself attain its aim. This dependence one upon the other for its natural existence is the basis of society.

The strength of an attachment is measured by the greatness of the desire and the ability and completeness of its gratification. Given two people each with a want the other is capable of supplying, the degree of satisfaction will depend upon the greatness of the want and the completeness of the interchange.

Human wants and desires are either physical or mental, or they are both of the body and of the mind. Purely physical wants are necessities and are required for the maintenance of a normal body. These are a proper amount of air, light, water, food, exercise, an harmonious adjustment with natural forces, etc.

Strictly mental desires are acquired, and are produced by previous education, training or experience. Among these may be mentioned the various anticipations, enthusiasms, ambitions, etc.

What concerns us most are those longings that are partly physical and partly mental. A new born babe has none but physical wants and its first movements are not controlled by will power at all, but are subject to reflex exclusively. For a short time after birth the conducting fibres between the undeveloped brain and the pyramidal fibres of the cord perform no functions. (Jacobi.) It takes the pyscho-motor centres a month to exhibit the first signs of existence. After a time the brain develops very fast but far from uniformly.

Since there are other than physical conditions which are agreeable and pleasing to us, pleasure becomes the gratification of the senses or of the mind. It naturally follows that the most complete satisfaction of the greatest physical and mental desires, occasions the supremest pleasure, which is synonymous with the fullest contentment.

Through the medium of the nervous system the mind obtains a knowledge of the existence both of the various parts and organs of the body, and of the external world. This knowledge is based upon sensations which result from the stimulation of certain centers, and these sensations are usually classed as "common" and "special."

Under the head of common sensations are placed all those general feelings which cannot be distinctly localized in any particular part of the body. Among these we have the muscular sense, and the sensations derived from the various viscera indicating the necessity of expelling their contents; the sense of fatigue, faintness, hunger, thirst, satiety, etc.

It is impossible to draw a very clear line of demarkation between many of the common sensations and those of a special nature. The sense of touch is usually classed with the "special" senses, yet it differs from them in being common to many nerves, and in its impressions being communicable through many organs. Like touch, the sexual sense might also be considered as one of the senses which partakes more or less of the "special" nature and still has "common" peculiarities. It might not inappropriately be considered the sixth sense.

The special senses must be developed, trained and educated to a degree of appreciation before pleasure will be obtained from their satisfaction. Hearing is that sense by which we distinguish sounds and are able to enjoy the charms of music and harmony, but we must first have learned to discriminate between noise and agreeable concords. An untrained child does not receive the pleasure from classical music that an educated musician enjoys because he does not possess the receptive capacity and hence has not the same desire. It requires a knowledge of language and rhetoric to be thrilled by the powers of oratory.

By the sense of sight we perceive the beauties of our surroundings as well as hideous things, and these are often pleasing or repugnant, according to the previous desires created in the mind of the individual. The surgeon witnesses a brilliant surgical operation with keen interest and satisfaction, while the same sight is quite enough to frequently be the cause of sickness when viewed by a sympathetic layman.

A familiar scene depicted upon canvas might cause a thrill of admiration, and awaken pleasant memories in the minds of the masses, while an artist would with disgust pronounce the painting a veritable daub.

The organs of smell and taste are situated at the entrance to the respiratory tract and alimentary canal and convey to the brain sensations that are agreeable or obnoxious, thereby enabling the person to avoid deleterious things as well as to seek those which give him pleasure. Previous experience gives the required knowledge and creates the desire which a discriminating judgment has learned to gratify. People with acquired tastes habitually eat not the requisite amount or the proper kind of food for the building up of the bodily tissues, but partake of enormous quantities of both solids and liquids because of the satisfaction of their sense of taste. Indeed, it is a common practice to indulge this sense to the limit of the physical capacity, and very frequently beyond.

By the faculty of attention the being can concentrate its thoughts and actions more or less exclusively upon any one of its senses and it is then more or less unconscious of the others. As every sensation is attended with an idea and leaves behind it an impression upon the mind which can be reproduced at will, we are enabled to compare the idea of a past sensation with another sensation really present. So long as the condition into which the stimulus has thrown the organ, endures, the sensation also remains, though the exciting cause should have long since ceased to act, for after-sensations are very vivid and durable.

By repeated and persistent use of the several senses there is recorded in the numberless recesses of the brain a fund of information which memory subsequently recalls, elaborates and utilizes. Mind, which may be considered the intellectual faculty in man, is extremely difficult of accurate definition and remains one of the great mysteries. It may, from one point of view, be said to be cerebration, or, what is evolved by the functioning of the brain. Certain it is that the minds of different people are as varied as their possessors, and since the brain is dependent upon the other structures of the body for its impressions, it may very largely be the result of cerebral stimulation.

The mental effect caused by the developed special senses seems to be in proportion to the development of these senses. Profound impressions conveyed to the brain by the special senses leave an indefinite imprint, and extraordinary sensations become ephemeral or enduring memories according to their intensity.

These special senses begin their development shortly after birth, and the mentality of the individual is very largely due to the facilities for their exercise, since previous experience creates the desire as well as gives knowledge from its gratification.

There is another factor, most often not sufficiently considered, which contributes perhaps more than these so-called special senses to the individuality and mental state of the person. This inherent and ever-present stimulus which constantly impresses and influences the brain to its recognition, is the sexual instinct, which is perceived and constitutes the sexual sense.

One has but to observe the very marked change in the thoughts, acts and conduct of the budding girl as she enters the transition to womanhood, to be fully convinced that her mental transformation is the direct result of her physical alterations. She finds herself possessed of an additional and new desire which is not the result of previous experience and education, but rather in spite of them, for it is inherent and elementary. So strong is this desire and so greatly does it influence the life of the girl that instead of nuturing and fostering its development, as is the case with the other senses, civilization and morality demand its curtailment, and eternal vigilance and unremitting restraint are enjoined and required for its subjection.

We may as well acknowledge that this is the "ruling passion" of adult life, for at all times and in all ages men have fought and women endured, while more sacrifices have been made for the sake of the feeling entertained by a member of one sex for a person of the opposite (regardless of what name may be applied to it) than for any other human attribute. Indeed, at certain periods in every life all other desires pale into insignificance when compared to this, the strongest, greatest and withal most vital and sacred of human longings.

At the age of puberty the physical changes in the boy make him distinctively masculine, while the bodily development of the girl causes a mentality and individuality that is decidedly feminine. This change is evidently due to the impressions conveyed to the brain from the differential organs, which gradually establish a consciousness that was hitherto unknown. In the natural order of things each sex is incapable, without the presence of the other, of indefinitely prolonging physical life, and this consciousness constitutes an affinity, one for the other, which is as constant and unerring as that mysterious force which causes the needle of the mariner's compass to forever be inclined toward the pole.

It is a truth that great preferences are entertained

for a certain one, and these are as varied as are the different people. This is eminently proper and indispensable to civilization, for without distinction there would be no morality, loyalty or virtue—the sublimest of human attributes. There can be nothing more admirable and ennobling, nor is there anything more conducive to the building of character than the devotion or affinity of the mature male, in the consciousness and glory of his manhood for the charming personality of an attractive femininity whose pronounced sexuality renders her adorable.

It is not so much the shape of the nose, the shade of the eyes, the color of the hair or the height of the stature that exerts the forceful influence—these are but auxiliaries to convey impressions—but rather the possession of a personality whose embodiment manifests a counterpart that is capable of transmitting concords to a personification responsively attuned. There is an attractive force which impells to the finding of that half of the whole whose eminences most accurately correspond to the natural depressions of the other, and whose approximation securely dovetails that superstructure upon which is builded the temple of human love. This powerful magnet is the sexual sense, by whose mystical influence our lives are shaped and guided, and than which none other so largely contributes to our several destinies nor makes or mars a happy, joyful and contented life.

This sense, like the others, is by cultivation refined, intensified and made remarkably discriminative; or by prolonged, habitual restriction and suppression a deficiency may be caused in the mental balance of people that should be considered morbid and eccentric.

It is a deep and discriminating knowledge of the psychology of man that requires the elimination of sexuality in order to insure a greater enthusiasm, deeper devotion and mental concentration for a spiritual cause. A keen observation of humankind doubtless prompted the poet to declare that some persons were "forever in a passion or a prayer."

The sexual sense and its development is a far greater causative factor in the production of mental states than is commonly supposed. Social commingling of the sexes leads to a well balanced mind, while too great intimacy, without proper exercise of the sexual function, often causes mental unbalance. It may be a great shock to romancers and sentimentalists to hear that individualized love is very largely a matter of propinquity, and is born and made enduring by being close to its object—but that does not disprove the fact.

The delights of association create attachments, and lonesomeness is caused by deprivation. In order to become homesick one must first have had a home. Only very imaginative persons become really infatuated without having been on terms of intimacy and having experienced the sensations incident to bodily proximity.

If two normally constituted adults of opposite sexes were to be isolated and removed from the possibility of meeting others, they would undoubtedly, if unrestrained, be prompted by their sexual sense and develop into lovers.

That the sexual sense has very much to do with a desirable condition of the mind is further abundantly proven by the fact that old maids and bachelors who abstain from natural sexual intercourse, are proverbially "cranky," eccentric and biased in their judgment.

A disposition is evinced even early in life to resent an intimation reflecting upon the sex of the person, and surgeons not infrequently encounter very old men who strenuously combat and resist to the last extremity, any proceeding tending to interfere with the prolongation of their sexual life.

Nothing so profoundly affects and depresses the mind of the average man for any length of time as the belief in his own sexual incompetence, even though it may be, as is most often the case, without foundation and wholly imaginative. A mere suggestion to credulous ones is often sufficient to shake the confidence in themselves that is required for equipoise; and this so greatly disturbs their tranquillity that they become easy victims to the prey of uncrupulous charlatans, who reap a bountiful harvest from the seed so ruthlessly sown. Any treatment, however absurd, which sufficiently affects the mind to restore the self-confidence is effective; for the mind and the sexual sense are so intimately entwined and blended that disturbance of one profoundly affects the other.

Additional proof that sexuality and psychic conditions are closely identified is found in the fact that persons who still retain some sense of honor and respectability, and who may have become infected with a venereal disease, very frequently suffer quite as much from remorse and self-reproach as from the pathological lesions incident to the disease. The great majority of people class venereal diseases among the most loathsome of affections, and have a horror for their contraction that serves to keep them from deviating from the path of rectitude.

It is difficult to conceive of a greater stigma being placed upon a person than to brand him or her as being possessed of a markedly different sexual sense than is felt by the majority of their kind, and those who have this knowledge guard their secret as sedulously almost as they do their very life; while the mentality of those who but entertain a suspicion that their sexuality is unlike those with whom they associate, is made morbid and only restored to a normal state when this suspicion has been removed.

CHAPTER II

SEXUAL PASSION

Passion is Exalted Feeling—Its Spontaneous Occurence—Aroused by Either Mental Impressions or Local Bodily Conditions—Cause of Imagination—Analysis of "Love at First Sight"—Ideal Sexual Love must be Both Mental and Physical—Ethics of Courtship—Pairing Hunger—Feelings Express a Desire for Excretion and Something More—Secrecy Clusters about Sexual Life—Emotion Creates Digust when not Responded To—Habits of Deception Instinctive and Required for Female Safety—What Men are Impelled to Give, Women Like to Receive—Sexual Perversion—Male Delights in Exerting Force and Domination; Female Derives Pleasure from Experiencing Force and Submission—Irresistible Women—Masculine Anger and Feminine Fear—Brain Center of Impulse and Nucleus for Romance—Cultivation of Ideas which Inhibit Desire—Self-induced Passion—Sexual Excitement During Sleep—Phenomena of Dreams—Nocturnal Emissions the Rule in Young Men, but Inexperienced Women Commonly have Vague Dreams—Causes of "Wet Dreams" and their Significance—Sexual Excitement During Sleep More Fatiguing—Woman's Dreams Tend to Reverberate Through Waking Hours—Sexual Needs of the Hysterical—Habits that Create Passion in the Female—Analysis of Day Dreams, Ravings, etc—Passion is Blind and Seeks to Grasp what Strikes Fancy.

Whenever any feeling or emotion more or less completely masters the mind we call it passion. The mind in such cases is considered as having lost its usual self-control and to have become the passive instrument of the feeling in question.

Sexual emotion or passion is an intensified feeling, and is the temporary heightening or exaltion of the natural physical and mental inclinations.

This condition is not characterized or made different by the nature of its object but is the result of its own nature.

By some means or other the mental concentration is directed to matters of sex, and when deeply immersed in its contemplations, the person is indifferent to the usual influences. We often, when in deep thought, have our eyes open and fixed but see nothing, because of the stimulus of ordinary light being unable to excite the brain to conceive when otherwise engaged.

When the stimulus has been sufficient to arouse an unusual activity, ordinary inhibition proves inadequate and the natural cravings become conspicuous.

There is more than one way by which the sexual sense is made especially manifest.

In healthy adults exalted sexual feeling occurs spontaneously at certain periods and under varying conditions, to a greater or lesser degree.

It is pretty generally conceded that about the period of menstruation in the female is a propitious time for its advent, while some attempts have been made to prove a periodicity in the male.

Aside from this natural tendency, there are two ways in which healthy adults are rendered what may be termed passionate, or in a state of sexual excitement. The one method is by mental impressions, and the other by local stimulation or irritation.

Two things will cause an excessive moisture in

the eye and bring forth tears—local irritation, as by a foreign body, and a profound mental impression. There are two methods of starting perspiration over the entire body—either severe physical or great mental activity or exertion. Vomiting may be caused in two ways—a local irritant, such as an emetic, or a disgusting sight or suggestion. Two things will excite the sexual apparatus to activity and cause the individual to become passionate—some form of local irritation or stimulation that causes hyperaemia; and the imagination, or mental impressions from without.

Imagination plays a very conspicuous role in the play of sexual emotions.

The so-called "Love at first sight" is a sudden and violent exaltation of the natural, inherent feeling, which a vivid imagination construes as having been awakened and intensified by its personified object. There is an abrupt consciousness of blissful ecstacy which the mind's eye conceives and imagines to be incorporated in the counterpart which seems so accurately fitted to conform to its own desires. The imagination associates its own intensified feelings with the coincident person and assumes that this particular one, above all others, is possessed of the requisites wherewith to satisfy its own longings, which have suddenly become forcibly awakened and are temporarily heightened.

When subsequent experience proves the inadequacy of the associated party to fulfill its fancied requirements, then comes disappointment and the ardor cools; whereas, if there be realization of fancied bliss and cherished hopes, the attachment continues and is augmented. We usually find that people who become suddenly smitten are comparatively inexperienced, have immature judgment or are prone to be uncommonly imaginative and excessively sentimental.

We have seen that the various involuntary physiological processes can be stimulated to increased activity in two different ways. Though sexual excitement may be induced by local irritation or may be of purely mental origin, yet it seems necessary, in order to maintain a healthy equipoise and to preserve a proper balance, that both should be taken into consideration and exercised in order to secure and maintain the nearest approach to ideal sexual love.

To those who are thoughtful and reflective it must be apparent that genuine love between the sexes can exist only when both the physical and the mental attributes of the person are considered, and the combined whole becomes the object of affection and adoration. There must be something tangible from which to draw the nourishment upon which affection feeds, and if the tree of adult human life is to flourish and be kept green, it must have its strongest and deepest root in the sensual element.

There must be a desire to be united with the beloved object and to possess its physical properties, with a view of rounding out a coupled or complete existence and fulfilling the laws of nature.

During sexual excitement there is not only a local physical manifestation, nor yet an affection of a nervous centre, but the entire vaso-motor nervous system is influenced. This involuntary system may be said to act as a medium which links the strictly physical with the purely mental being, and if the desire be manifested and limited to either one alone, it must be to the detriment of the other.

In other words, an attraction that is wholly physical cannot be conducive to a tranquil mind, and leads to unbalance; while a purely mental affinity without any bodily attractiveness permits of no physical activity to perform a physiological function, and so destroys necessary harmony, which is a fundamental requisite to a normal state.

Platonic love, pure and simple, is mental affinity only, and does not take physical attractions or sensations into consideration, nor does it include the sexual relation, which is perhaps the chief factor that contributes to the attraction. It does not mean all of the feelings that members of one sex have for those of the opposite, and, therefore, does not express in its entirety what constitutes the love of normal adults, and hence is but another term for friendship.

On the other hand, when merely the body of the person is the object of desire and sensual pleasure the sole aim, there is an incompleteness resulting, which, when the force of the passion has been exhausted, prevents the bond from becoming constant and enduring; and this condition likewise should not be termed love, as it is only lust.

Under our present social conditions mutual love (which is only conceivable in a normal way as existing between two individuals of opposite sex who are capable of sexual intercourse) is usually developed into its true and pure form by the ethics of courtship.

Favorable mental impressions lead to the cultivation of social intercourse, and proximity, by the aid of imagination, gradually develops an agreeable association. Yielding to natural inclinations, each is impressed with the other's ability to supply what is deemed needful for contentment, until finally it becomes apparent that their union is essential to their happiness. A conviction of this desirable condition is considered as proof of their being in "love," which is the holy aspiration of every normal human being.

Without sexual excitement, or passion, union of the sexes could not be accomplished, for the physical conditions are such that there are general and vascular changes in the system, and the whole being is affected.

Ziegler maintains that "In all animals a high degree of excitement of the nervous system is necessary to procreation, and thus we find an excited prelude to procreation widely spread." The condition has been said to have for its purpose the production of a pairing hunger, and be a state of profound and explosive irritability which has for its mental antecedent and concomitant an irresistible craving.

Prof. Morgan observes, "The hypothesis of sexual selection suggests that the accepted mate is the one which adequately evokes the pairing impulse. Courtship may thus be regarded from a physiological point of view as a means of producing the requisite amount of pairing hunger (sexual passion); and courtship is thus the strong and steady bending of the bow that the arrow may find its mark in a biological end of the highest importance in the survival of a healthy and vigorous race."

There is a certain similarity between the exalted sexual feeling and the impulse to evacuate an excretion. It is not to be supposed that the expulsion of a little mucus, such as occurs from the female genital tract during contact, would be attended with such profound mental agitation as accompanies sexual excitement if the only object was an excretory one.

The fluids emitted during an orgasm are not waste material and their retention would in themselves not be altogether a disadvantage, while the evacuations of the bladder and bowls are deleterious to the system and their expulsion is demanded.

The preliminaries to the sexual act, or the conditions which constitute passion, are in civilized human beings sometimes in themselves a partial satisfaction to the sexual impulse, and though the desire may simulate a bodily need for excretion, yet the feeling expresses this want and something in addition.

There must be a line of demarkation between the normal and abnormal sexual inclinations, but this line is difficult to draw; and owing to the general social attitude toward matters sexual, and especially to certain practices, every person who possess a feeling of pride, be it ever so small, is impelled by his or her consciousness and dread of inviting opprobrium, to at least remain silent, if not to misrepresent, in regard to their true sexual status.

There is no one but has some secret, small though it may be, which they cannot bring themselves to divulge, and if there is anything in this world around which secrecy clusters, it is about the sexual life.

There is a tendency among intelligent people to

appear, in their calm and rational moments, what they are led to believe will meet with the approval of the desirable persons with whom they come in contact, even to the point of simulating a sexual condition they do not really feel.

In the case of the female it usually consists in the suppression of the natural emotion, together with a denial of its existence, or at least a reticence to acknowledge the exact condition, which is taken to imply its absence. Among males a like impression is considered a reflection upon manhood and usually looked upon as a deficiency or weakness.

The general social attitude is such that a show of sexual feeling or aptitude on the part of woman invites adverse criticism from her kind; while an intimation of the lack of virility in the male shakes self-confidence and provokes resentment.

It is a matter of frequent observance that between the two sexes, physical manifestations of sexual emotion tend to inspire disgust in a person who is not inclined to respond to them—however salutary and delightful this show of feeling may be at the proper time with the right and fit party.

Habit, which is an acquired involuntary tendency to do that which was originally purely voluntary, is to a considerable extent responsible for our several conditions and actions.

When the wisdom of an observing man prompted the declaration that "all men are liars,' he uttered what seems to prevail throughout the whole of animal life, whenever self-protection and the sexual relation are involved.

Deception for the purpose of self-preservation is instinctive, and when it comes to the practical sexual life of the female, it may be said that woman's ability in this respect is greater than the man's. "All is fair in love and war," is an axiom that serves as a practical guide for conduct and seems by implication to be a mutual agreement.

The corrections and chastisements of childhood lead to the habit of concealing that which meets with censure, but which cannot in the nature of things be avoided.

A show of sexual feeling, except under the prescribed conditions, nearly always meets with a reprimand and hence it is habitually disguised or suppressed.

The female is called upon, for her own protection, to dissimulate and deceive regarding her sexual passion, for in addition to the animal instinct she will, by reason of her experience and observation since early childhood, have acquired habits of strategy and will exercise tact, with more or less discretion, when her natural feelings may become emphasized.

Her moral training dictates the right to mislead for the benefit of what is considered to be of advantage to society, and her physical safety demands a disguise of passion in order to insure her security from attack.

Morally, as well as in conformity to the part which nature designed that she should play in the material world, it is to her disadvantage to actively display sexual emotion as such.

When the sexual passion becomes aroused only

by extreme and extraordinary means, the normal limit has been passed and the condition is termed perversion or the person is called a sexual pervert.

What men are ordinarily impelled to give, women usually like to receive, but there is now and again a case in which the sexual impulse consists in a tendency to maltreat or abuse the beloved person, as an association of violence and cruelty with sexual excitement or enjoyment seems necessary. This condition is known as Sadism and these perverts sometimes commit frightful and shocking acts. The opposite extreme is known as Masochism and is described by Krafft-Ebing as follows: "By Masochism I understand a peculiar perversion of the physical vita *sexualis* in which the individual affected, in sexual feeling and thought, is controlled by the idea of being completely and unconditionally subject to the will of a person of the opposite sex, of being treated by this person as by a master, humiliated and abused. This idea is colored by sexual feeling; the Masochist lives in fancies in which he creates situations of this kind, and he often attempts to realize them."

A third kind of perversion is known as homosexuality, in which a person is attracted, excited by, and in love, with a member of the same sex, and who seeks sexual enjoyment in this manner only.

Within normal limits a little pain sometimes acts as an excitant to passion, for it is one of the most powerful methods of arousing emotion. The male finds some pleasure in exerting force and has a tendency to delight in domination, but the female derives some pleasure in experiencing force and tends to delight in submission. One of the common love dreams of a young woman is a position in which she fancies herself abandoned to her lover, as being able to rely upon his physical and mental strength, as being swept beyond the control of her own will and being in delightful submission to one that is stronger. For the average woman there is something fascinating in "the lover's pinch, which hurts and is desired."

The normal man does not wish to be cruel, and a little pain is often inflicted in kindness, though not in anger; but when it is carried beyond the limits which he knows he can himself soothe, it is no longer enjoyed.

A woman often in the ecstacy of passion, implores a man to desist, though that is really the last thing she desires, and a man who fails to realize this has not progressed very far in the art of love making.

The maiden dislikes the idea of being too easily won and she gives more pleasure also to her lover than one who yields at once.

There is something apparently contradictory in a woman's emotions, for the maternal instinct craves something innocent and helpless, which she may cherish and protect; while the sexual instinct delights in something bold, audacious or reckless, and she is not perfectly happy in her lover unless he satisfies to some extent each of these two opposite longings.

Those women who obtain extraordinary sway over men are apparently those who possess a certain "virility," or procreative and copulative aptitude in their character and passions. "If with this *virility* they combine a fragility or childishness of appearance, which appeals to a man in another way at the same time, they appear to be irresistible," observes a lady writer.

The emotions of fear and anger are somewhat allied to the sexual passion and may reinforce its active power. In the more primitive life, courtship with the female is a skillful manipulation of her own fears, and with the male it is largely a display of combativity.

Masculine anger and feminine fear serve to arouse the being from a state of lethargy and cause excitement and activity, and though their initial stage may be disagreeable, they are often not avoided but even deliberately sought on account of the emotional waves they occasion. These emotions gorge the muscular systems with blood and put them in better fighting trim.

Courage is the essential male characteristic of which love is the reward, and in order to succeed in love, fear must be overcome in the male as well as the female. In the same way pain is not unwelcome, for it acts as a sexual stimulent because it is an efficacious method of stirring up animation.

The brain is supposed to contain an area which, when stimulated, causes sexual passion. This portion of the cerebrum has not been positively located but it is probable that a region of the cortex acts as a center from which arises sexual impulse and excitement.

Spontaneous sexual life has its beginning in the orgnic sensations which arise from development of the sexual organs, and which commands the attention of the individual. These sensations are pleasurable and the impressions are converted into more or less clear ideas which are associated with, and accentuated by, the experiences of every day life.

With this nucleus romance is built, and wonderful tales and situations are constructed by the imagination, which serve to entertain and amuse, and which always gravitate to the interesting topic of love.

The brain center is stimulated, the organism excited and the person made passionate by means of the memory, the perceptions of sight, the impressions of touch, and, in a minor degree, sometimes by association with the senses of smell and hearing.

When any one thing serves as an excitant to the exclusion of all others it is termed a "fetich," or an artificial source of enthusiasm, but this unreasonable source of passion is beyond the mark which designates the normal.

Under normal conditions the brain center responds to the various stimulations of the special senses, and though one of these may at times become accentuated yet all of them contribute somewhat to the influence of excitability.

The reading of suggestive literature or the inspection of lascivious pictures attracts the mind to sexual things and awakens memories that bring on an exalted feeling. The sight of a person of the opposite sex with bewitching eyes, pretty teeth, rosy complexion, beautiful hair, well developed physique, etc., often impresses the center and occasions passion. Touching hands, petting, fondling and kissing another when there is a possibility of sexual relations, nearly always awakens sexual excitement. The hearing of an agreeable voice or some kinds of music, and the odors of some varieties of perfumes or flowers are more or less suggestive to some persons and have their influence in creating passion. All of these, severally or combined, may impress and influence the mind to unusual activity and concentration, and the whole organism responds and is rendered sexually passionate.

The sexual feeling may be considered as composed of impressions which spring from the center or come from the periphery, and also the pleasurable feelings which are associated with these perceptions.

The longing for sexual satisfaction arises from this general conception and the desire grows stronger in proportion as the cerebral center accentuates the feeling and the erection center increases the sensation.

The brain, by appropriate concepts, and by exercise of the imagination, increases the longing; and the excitation of the erection center, with the consequent congestion of the genital organs, increases the sensations to lustful feelings.

If conditions are favorable for satisfactory copulation, the constantly increasing desire is complied with; but if inhibitory circumstances arise, the sexual longing is overcome and the act is prevented.

Natural and physical conditions have a marked influence and effect upon the instinctive impulse, while education and the cultivation of self-control give a decisive influence and inhibitory power to the mind.

Civilized society requires the cultivation of a readiness with the ideas which inhibit sexual desire. The moral teachings are such that a yielding to passion is considered bad for the individual as well as society, and this leads to the commendable cultivation of control in this respect.

The discipline to which the person is subjected creates judgment, which decides between what is proper and good, and what is improper and bad.

When the sexual promptings are recognized there arises a question for decision, and the point to be determined is whether or not to yield to passionate desire.

The decision depends, on the one hand, upon the strength of the natural impulse, together with the coincident physical sensations; and, on the other hand, upon the power of the inhibitory influences.

If reason dictates that under some circumstances violence or wrong would be committed by progress, and self-control be sufficient to overcome the impulse, then there would be inhibition of progress and passion would be subdued.

The exciting and inhibitory powers vary with the individual and also with the circumstances.

Intoxication has a marked effect upon these forces, as it awakens and increases the longing for satisfaction and at the same time reduces the moral resistance.

There is also a difference in the sexes regarding these powers.

Practically the moral phase is made to appeal more strongly to the female and increases her inhibitory propensities, while the active part which the male is called upon by nature to play increases the force of his impulses.

Spontaneous sexual excitement frequently arises

from the organism itself, and transformations of repressed sexual activity are a factor of some morbid conditions, as well as the usual manifestations of art, poetry, etc., and it may be said that its workings color, more or less, the whole of life.

We are disposed to look only upon the surface, and hence see nothing but the results which arise from subconscious, or involuntary mentality.

The exalted sexual impulse is frequently manifest when the mind is in abeyance and the person is asleep.

During sleep there is a suspension of the bodily and mental powers, in which the consciousness is without the guidance and data of the will and lower centers, and hence the functions are performed illogically.

There are, however, very different degrees of sleep in different parts of the nervous system, and these differences bring about the phenomena of dreams.

During a dream the brain is still partially active but the mind products of its action are no longer corrected by impressions of objects belonging to the outer world. A dream is physiologically defined as unconscious cerebration, in which there is a series of thoughts without the mental process of reasoning.

Dreams of a sexual nature are common and very generally experienced. They occur with varying degrees of vividness and the impressions upon the waking hours are variable.

Sexual dreams in women who have never experienced an orgasm when awake, are usually of a very vague kind.

It is not, as a rule, until the orgasm—under

whatever conditions it may have been produced—has been experienced in the waking state, that it begins to occur in women during sleep, and even then it is probably less frequent than in the other sex.

While it is the rule for the young man who has been continent to have sexual excitement with emission while asleep, it is the exception for the chaste maiden to have dreams which are of a distinctly sexual nature and in which there are the sensations of sexual excitement and orgasm.

Young women often have dreams, from which they are sometimes suddenly awakened, which are prompted by the sexual feeling but which amount to nothing more than impulses.

The sensations and thoughts in these cases are disconnected, and not coherent, and do not develop to the extent of being a definite and vivid dream, but terminate in vagueness.

In the male, this phenomenon usually appears about the time of puberty and continues at intervals of varying duration during sexual life, according to whether or not sexal relations are had.

The ejaculation is generally, though not always, accompanied by dreams in which there are sexual sensations which lead up to the climax, and its occurrence is influenced, more or less, by physical, mental or emotional excitement; local inflammatory conditions; the state of the bladder; the position in bed; the taking of stimulents, etc.

The reflex center for ejaculation has been shown by Budge to be situated at the level of the fourth lumbar vertebra, and when the stimulus has been sufficient to excite this center to activity, the center acts and emission occurs.

All in all, it is a fairly general, definite and regular phenomenon, realized upon awakening and followed by a conscious sense of dissatisfaction, sometimes a little fatigue and occasionally some depression or headache.

Practically all celibate men have such emissions, and when they do not occur more often than on an average of approximately once a week, the condition may be considered as the usual one.

It is the frequency of their occurrence and not the occasional happening that should suggest an abnormal state and lead to a removal of those conditions which favor their production.

To be sure, sexual activity during sleep cannot be satisfactory, and it is often disgusting and revolting, though it has sometimes been found to be refreshing.

Many men and women can bear witness that sexual excitement during sleep is more fatiguing than when it occurs in the waking state, though this does not always obtain.

Nocturnal sexual excitement in women is comparatively infrequent, for some strongly sexual women who have been compelled to relapse into a repressed life experience it only on rare occasions and at long intervals.

It presents a peculiarity in that these dreams are in women more readily prolonged into the conscious state and tend to reverberate through the waking hours.

Some instances have been recorded in which such dreams have been considered a reality, and this should suggest to the physician the advisability, for his own protection, of having another woman or at least a friendly third party present when an anæsthetic is administered, as that is a favorable time for such an occasion, and the dream may be so vivid as to make the patient believe she has had sexual congress.

This tendency has been frequently observed in healthy women and it sometimes becomes exaggerated to a high degree in neurotic subjects.

That these dreams may become day-time delusions is strikingly shown by the "Psychology of Sex," in which is published a communication by an intelligent and clever, though neurotic, young woman, who writes: "For years I have been trying to stamp out my passional nature, and was beginning to succeed when a strange thing happened to me last autumn. One night, as I lay in my bed, I felt an influence so powerful that a man seemed present with me. I crimsoned with shame and wonder. I remember that I lay upon my back, and marveled when the spell had passed. The influence, I was assured, came from a priest whom I believed in and admired above everyone in the world. I had never dreamed of love in connection with him, because I always thought him so far above me. The influence has been upon me ever since—sometimes by day and nearly always by night; from it I generally go into a deep sleep, which lasts until morning. I am always much refreshed when I wake. This influence has the best effect upon my life that anything has ever had as regards health and mind. It is the knowledge that I am loved fittingly that makes me so indifferent to my future. What worries me is that I sometimes wonder if I suffer from a nervous disorder merely."

To be held responsible for some action when the possibility of exerting influence or control has been removed, as is the case when one is asleep, is manifestly unjust.

This tendency which sexual excitement during sleep has to influence the waking emotions and actions, is seen in an extreme form in hysterical women, in whom the sensations are often painful.

The occurrence of pain in the place of agreeable voluptuous sensations, is explained upon the hypothesis that there is a conflict between the physical impulses and the mental attitude.

When the mere physical impulse is strong enough to assert itself in spite of the mental emotions and abhorrence, the illusion of sexual intercourse provokes pain. The sexual needs of the hysterical are equally as individual and various as are those of normal women, but they suffer from them through a moral struggle with the instinct and try to keep them in the background.

It is probable, however, that the painfulness of hysterical manifestations is magnified and more often apparent than real, as it may be nothing more than repugnance for the physical aspect of passion.

Some of the common habits or occupations of women tend to produce conditions in which there is sexual excitement and orgasm in both the waking and sleeping state.

Riding in a railway train or other conveyance with somewhat of a vibratory motion, sometimes occasions excitement, especially when sitting so as to be leaning forward. Riding a bicycle or running a sewing machine tends, by the movements of the lower limbs and the friction occasioned, to sometimes produce such a condition of the genital organs as to lead to excitement, and even orgasm.

In some cases nothing but the pressure of the thighs, which is more or less voluntarily brought to bear upon the sexual region, is required to bring excitement, for some women can "hold themselves" so as to call it forth at will. Sitting or standing with the limbs firmly crossed and then rocking the pelvis so that the genitals are pressed against the thighs, sometimes occasions eroticism in the female as well as in the male. These, as well as thoughts and sensory impressions, more or less frequently awaken passion or pave the way for sexual excitement during sleep.

There is another condition which is not excitement nor yet complete abeyance of the sexual impulse, but which occurs most often during the period of adolescence and is not recognized as being of a sexual origin or nature.

The condition is found in refined and imaginative young people who lead chaste lives and would be repelled by thoughts and acts of a sexual nature, if they knew them to be such. It occurs most often in girls and young women, but it is occasionally seen in the other sex, and though it is not by any means always due to the sexual promptings, yet it may be said that this impulse is frequently a factor in its production.

This accentuation or transitional stage between the sexual instinct and passion, is shown by the so-called day dreams, reveries or ravings, which are most frequently encountered in romantic young women.

Such dreams are developed in solitude and secrecy and from a personal pleasurable basis. They originate from some incident and sometimes develop from the thoughts of a kiss to voluptuous gratification. The climax is usually brought about in accordance with the person's growing experience and personal knowledge. There is unwillingness and difficulty in putting into language what is evoked, which is of a romantic and dramatic character. These solitary reveries often cause genital congestion or even, in pronounced cases, spontaneous orgasm.

It may be considered a rather usual accompaniment of the subject's age and becomes abnormal only when in extreme form.

The sexual feeling is by no means always involved, but a significance of its sexual origin may be found in the observation that even when these dreams are not colored by sexual matters, the condition frequently ceases altogether upon marriage.

When it is recognized that passion is inherent and is in itself blind, but furiously and impetuously pushes out without calculation or comprehension of its object, to anything which the imagination deems fitted to its needs; and when the foregoing statements are given due consideration, it is little wonder that the average individual should be in ignorance of or have an erroneous conception of what the normal sexual condition of a fellow being actually is.

The existing social state precludes the probability of ascertaining definite knowledge upon this most vital topic, which must needs cause grave apprehension in the minds of intelligent, thoughtful and reflective men and women.

CHAPTER III

FEMALE SEXUAL SENSE

Feeling of Shame Taught—Primary Causes of Modesty are Animal and Social; the Principal Factors, Fear and Disgust—Excretions of Body are Offensive—Menstrual Flow Obnoxious and Evidences Hidden—Social Customs Inhibit or Extend Physical Display—Conscious Violation of Proprieties the Cause of Shame—Expectation of Modesty Provokes it—Nature's Coupling of the Center of Attraction with Physical Repugnance Creates Coquetries—How Modesty is Overcome—Influence of Intoxication—Sexual Congress only Way of Satisfying Reproductive Desire—Female Attitude is Passive, but not without Exerting Force—Man's Failure to Take Initiatory Step Makes Woman Active—Three Primary Sexual Centers—Feelings of Sexual Origin Gratified in Other Ways—Women Regard Mental Aspect of Devotion of Greatest Importance—Spontaneous Desire—Restraining Influence of Menstruation—Ardor Gradually Increased by Relations—Passivity Passes into Eager Participation During Intercourse—Physical State of Sexual Excitement—The Ideal Woman Not Without Passion—Suppression of Feeling—Higher Education and Marriage—Solitary Sexual Practices in Women.

One of the first things that a mother seeks to instill into the mind of her little girl, is a feeling of shame which centers about the pelvic organs and their functions.

This feeling, together with shyness, bashfulness, timidity, etc., develops a modesty which constitutes one of the chief, if not the greatest, of feminine charms. The mother is paving the way for her daughter's future happiness, for this commendable virtue not only acts as a shield and protection to the girl, but, by giving play to the imagination, provides for the happiness of her future lover.

It has been said that "Modesty is the mother of love," and its powers are so great that when a tender woman betrays herself with her lover it is done by deeds rather than by words.

There may, unfortunately perhaps, be an evil aspect in that it constantly leads to deception and falsehood and necessitates the penetration of the veil that is so effectively thrown over the sexual promptings, if one is to ascertain the true and natural condition.

When we come to study and analyze modesty, which may be said to be an almost instinctive prompting to concealment, that usually centers about the sexual processes, we find it common to both sexes but more peculiarily feminine.

We feel constrained to coincide with the view of Havelock Ellis that modesty has both an animal and a social basis, the principal factors of which are fear and disgust.

Throughout the whole animal kingdom the female is the passive and the male the active party in matters sexual.

It is only at certain periods that the female animal permits sexual congress, and this periodicity varies in different animals.

The female invites or entices the male to sexual activity only during the rutting season, while at all other times she is impelled, to shield herself from harm, to assume an attitude of sexual refusal.

In order to excite the male she feigns an unwillingness, during the period of sexual inclination, which is more apparent than real, and this show of antagonism serves to stimulate an eagerness in the male which is desirable. She tantalizes him by resistance and flees with the expectation of pursuit, for when she runs it is "in a circle" as it were, with the hope of being overtaken; but when caught she readily submits.

It should be remembered that sexual desire in the female animal is always spontaneous and subject to a definite periodicity.

The above is susceptible of such abundant proof that argument is deemed unnecessary.

This same animal trait or characteristic is found in the human female, and this instinctive prompting to conceal sexual willingness enters very largely into the causation of modesty.

Venus, the goddess of love and emblem of womanly modesty, is depicted in an attitude of sexual refusal, in which the sexual centers are shielded from approach, with one hand protecting the breast and the other guarding the pubic region from invasion.

The male being aggressive and the female function being periodic, this attitude of modesty becomes an involuntary expression of the organic fact that copulation is decidedly limited.

This defensive attitude of the female, being of necessity almost constant, becomes so habitual that it encroaches upon the few moments when it ceases to be in place, and this fact has called forth the statement by Scott that "the feeling of shame is made to be overcome."

One of the most universal social characteristics of man is the aptitude for disgust, which Richet says is evoked by the dangerous and the useless.

The secretions, and especially the excretions of the digestive and sexual organs, being useless and more or less dangerous to man, makes them disgusting, and that part of the anatomy from which they come ordinarily produces a similar feeling; hence the acts of evacuation are private and the parts kept secret, as their publicity provokes disgust.

Even among men exhibitions of the anal region and examinations of the rectum are complied with only when the most urgent necessity demands it, as it is suggestive of dirtiness and the patients are possessed of a feeling that they are subjecting the doctor to insult and are degrading themselves when soliciting such a procedure.

This same feeling of shyness and diffidence obtains to a great extent in cases of venereal disease.

In women the period of menstruation suggests uncleanness and the mestrual discharge is regarded as especially obnoxious, and in some instances contaminating, while it is truly remarkable how successfully women suppress evidences of this essentially physiological feminine function.

It is noteworthy that even mothers very reluctantly talk freely with their own daughters upon this subject, for very many girls receive but meager, if any, instructions from the proper source, and if the curiosity of the growing girl at her crucial period of life is not actually met with a reprimand she is frequently put off with a few words as to her personal care.

So completely is evidence of menstruation removed that most everyone learns nothing about this matter except by hearsay, for it is usually by this method alone that knowledge of its occurrence is obtained.

The same fear of evoking disgust deters women from permitting examinations of their genitalia and even abandoned women-of-the-half-world will not permit more than casual inspection of their privates; for minute examination is given only to the physician when necessity requires.

These elements of fear and disgust give to the genito-anal region a privacy and create for this portion of the anatomy a concentrated focus of reticence, or modesty.

Another very considerable circumstance in the production of modesty is the social factor.

Custom and fashion in civilized countries can easily inhibit anatomical modesty and quite as readily extend or accentuate any physical display.

A young society belle will with impunity parade in bathing costume on the beach at a watering place, or appear in a ball-room attired in garments that display portions of her anatomy which she would blush to exhibit in a park or public thoroughfare. The sight of a woman of refinement in her nightrobe, though it be very pretty and elaborate and effectively conceal her figure, will cause her great discomfiture, while a very liberal display of her shapely nether extremities encased in tights when she participates in a tableau for charitable purposes gives her evident pleasure and satisfaction.

It is the consciousness of violating proprieties that causes her shame and not her own sensibilities, for if she conducts herself in accordance with what she is convinced is expected of her, she has no scruples.

This is illustrated further by the fact that in confinements and diseases of women if the doctor is timid and approaches the woman with the evident expectation of being shocked, she is pretty certain to become so; whereas, if she is impressed and made to realize that whatever is done is proper and necessary under the circumstances, it almost invariably happens that modesty at once disappears.

To state it differently, if one is too careful to guard the modesty of a woman, she will be careful also; but if it be not unduly considered and she be convinced that it is not expected, modesty vanishes.

Blushing is the sanction of modesty, and is evidence that there is something to conceal which it is feared may be discovered. It is an emotional confusion arising from fear of detection, and to some extent people are modest because they feel the possibility of blushing, rather than that they blush because they are modest.

The influence of darkness in restraining the manifestation of modesty is well known to all lovers. Girls cover their faces with their hands but look through their fingers when prompted to get a peek at things sexual.

The fear of causing disgust, together with the fear of violating social etiquette and that of destroying or losing sexual allurements, constitutes the greatest part of modesty.

The fact that nature has coupled the great center of physical attraction with physical repugnance has made woman mysterious, coquetries possible and courtship complex.

This fact may also be of service in demonstrating that clothing serves a two-fold purpose—that of covering and protecting, and that of adornment.

The foregoing leads to the conclusion that whatever stimulates self-confidence and allays the fear of arousing disgust, has a tendency to banish and overcome modesty.

To correctly study the female sexual sense one must understand and properly regard feminine modesty, than which there is no more charming, admirable, or ennobling womanly virtue.

The presence of a beloved person in whom complete confidence is felt and in whose good opinion there is every assurance of steadfast continuance, seems to be necessary to overcome feminine modesty, and to permit a woman to act in accordance with her true and natural promptings and inclinations without restrictions.

Absolute freedom from restraint is probably very rarely attainable in a quiescent state, nor does this condition ever obtain in the presence of a third party. Moreover, the faculty of putting into words and accurately expressing one's true inwardness is given to but very few, while those who possess this ability are, owing to the many exigencies, loath to exercise it.

The narcotizing influence of slight intoxication,

as well as the deadening effect of insanity, tend to lull the manifestation of modesty and may serve to aid us in the study of this interesting topic.

Ordinarily we are beset with many difficulties and are constantly struck when seeking knowledge upon sexuality, with the applicability of the assertion of Talleyrand that, with regard to the sexual life at least, "Speech was not given to people to express their thoughts, but to disguise them."

Starting with the fact that the desire for reproduction, (which finds satisfaction in sexual congress, and which is obtained in no other way) is inherent and fundamentally a part of mature woman, as well as a full-grown cell, we find that early in life differences in sex become manifest.

The little girl thinks a great deal of her dollie and spends many hours playing the little mother.

There are other things that are essentially girlish that occur at this time of life but which need not take our attention. It is at the time of puberty that there is a great change in the mentality, actions and physical structure on the giowing girl.

The breasts begin to develop at this time, hair makes its appearance on the pubes, there is a change in the generative organs and menstruation begins to appear. Her thoughts are directed into other chancls; curiosity regarding sexuality supervenes, and altogether the advent and circumstances of menstruation linger long in the memory of the woman.

About this time, and perhaps for a considerable period thereafter, the sexual emotion has not become centered in the sexual organs.

It is probable that not until the time when a woman has actual sexual experience in a natural and physiological way does she come to understand, realize or appreciate the origin and significance of sexual emotion.

Sexual impulse or emotion varies greatly in women, and even in the same woman at different ages and periods.

The most divergent opinions are entertained relative to the feminine sexual impulse, and there are those who hold that sexual anæsthesia should be considered as natural in women, and maintain that any other opinion would be degrading; while others who do not share this opinion believe that sexual frigidity among civilized women is unnaturally prevalent.

Those extremists who hold that sexual impulse in woman is degrading should remember that the movements of the bowels and evacuations of the bladder are not agreeable to contemplate, though they are necessary to life and are attended with satisfaction and a degree of gratification to the individual.

The exercise and satisfaction of the reproductive function ought certainly, to say the very least, be equally as gratifying; and when we come to consider that this act is not only the supreme fact and symbol of love but also the supreme creative act, we cannot but acknowledge that, under normal conditions, it must be the most satisfying and most pleasurable of all acts.

If it were not so it would be contrary and in opposition to all nature, and if that action by which all human beings must come to this world be a degradation and can not be anticipated with the greatest pleasure, nor consummated with supremest bliss, then, indeed, must our mothers be disgraced and the race become extinct.

A fundamental character of the female sexual attitude is that of passivity, which is a purely natural sexual difference. The part played by the female in courtship is one of apparent antagonism to the aggressiveness of the male, but instead of the seeming inactivity having a repellant force it in reality exerts an attraction that is forceful.

The coyness of the female, like the male aggressiveness, is unconsciously assumed and most effectively brings about the ultimate union of the sexes.

The male naturally takes the initiative, but there is also an attractive force which acts like a magnet and draws him to the seemingly passive female.

The woman in love does not solicit by words the advances of her lover, but there is a language of the eyes whose muteness appeals and extends the invitation, and there is an intense energy behind, which is absorbed and pre-occupied in the end to be attained.

She awaits the movement of the natural aggressor, but if he fails to act, she heself essays to move, and does appear to shun, in order to entice.

It has previously been stated that about the time of puberty the female sexual emotion has not become centered in the sexual organs and hence the girl does not understand her feelings, which are not rarely diverted into other channels.

The immense social force at work may, during these years compel the girl to an unnatural extension of her already passive part, and thus the sexual impulse becomes latent and is with difficulty called forth, if at all.

In a considerable number of women this impulse remains dormant until aroused by the caresses of a lover. It has been said that "the youth spontaneously becomes a man; but the maiden must be kissed into a woman."

The sexual mechanism in women is much more complex than in men, and because it is natural for the male to take the initial step in the preparation for union, the function of the male to arouse the feminine impulse closely borders upon the normal.

This complexity makes the female mechanism susceptible to more frequent disturbance and causes a simulation of frigidity, or organic coldness, which is very deceptive to many.

The complex sexual apparatus of the female also causes the sexual impulse to be more extensive and more diffused. Instead of having one primary sexual focus as the male, woman has at least three sexual centers—the clitoris, the vaginal passage and the breasts, or more particularly the nipple.

There are other secondary and reflex centers in both sexes, but the three just enumerated give to the woman a much greater magnitude and wider sphere of emotion than is commonly realized.

Owing to this diffused character of the female sexual emotions it often happens that feelings which have a sexual origin are not recognized as such by the women themselves, and they find an equivalent in allied manifestations of enthusiasm.

A woman can find a certain gratification in a number of ways that do not include the sexual act proper, because the mental state may have a physical origin and basis in a center remote from the generative organs.

Women as a rule generally regard the mental aspect of devotion as of greater importance than do men, for they obtain a degree of gratification from actions that are not strictly sexual.

A woman lays more stress upon the preliminary caresses to the sexual act proper than does the man, because of the greater diffusion of the sexual zones; and she tends to be more emotional from the fact that the areas from where these sensations arise are more widespread.

A suggestive kiss or gentle stroking of the spine awakens pleasurable emotions, while manipulations of the bust and tender caresses centering about the nipple cause hyperæmia of the generative organs and call forth sexual excitement in the woman, though titillation of the nipple in the man has practically no sexual significance.

The sexual impulse in women shows a very much greater tendency to be periodic than it does in men. It not only is less apt to so frequently occur spontaneously, but this occurrence is markedly related to menstruation.

The mental condition of a woman is greatly influenced by her monthly periods and this fact may account for the origin of the assertion that "A woman's mind is in her womb."

Most women, and especially those who have had

sexual experience, have some degree of sexual desire just before, during or after their menstrual periods.

A woman may have intense sexual feelings about the time of her menstrual period and remain perfectly tranquil and self-possessed during the rest of the month. These spontaneous periods of emotion, which are more peculiarly feminine, are physiological and have their basis in the hyperæmic condition of the sexual organs at this time.

Women whose mental activity may sometimes seem to be limited and who then appear to be listless and rather inert, become, when their sexual emotions are kindled, full of life and activity. That emotion which, it might sometimes be said to unmake the man, makes the woman truly herself.

We often wonder at the power and influence exerted by a woman who is dull and mediocre, who by the world at large is considered commonplace; and we find a solution of the problem in the fact that for the man with whom she is in love she becomes transformed and enlivened, for he sees what is hidden from all others.

It has been stated in a foregoing paragraph that the time when a woman is most apt to become sexually emotional is just before, during and after the menstrual period. To people of refinement the menstrual discharge is repugnant and this consciousness tends to prohibit sexual intercourse at this time. This conviction brings about a mental restraint that tends to lessen the heightening of desire, and thus it is that spontaneous sexual emotion is commonly more marked immediately after and before menstruation.

Many women who are forced to abstain from sexual relations and who are not disturbed by this impulse during the remainder of the month, find relief from the nervousness of their emotional state at this time by in some other manner bringing about a nervous explosion.

Owing to the definite periodicity of the female impulse, as well as its comparative lack of simplicity, sexual desire and excitement in the female requires to be more frequently actively aroused.

The ardor of the emotion tends to be gradually increased after relations have been established, and the climax, or sexual orgasm, is not reached as quickly in the female as in the male.

During normal intercourse the apparent passivity of the female, which is often associated with physical and moral sensitiveness, passes into a stage of active participation and assistance in the performance of the act.

If for any reason progress is retarded on the part of the woman, and the process be unequally progressive, as when her submission is a deliberately willful act instead of being instinctive and impulsive, there must of necessity be failure of sexual relief and gratification.

In other words, there will be disappointment, for the same act which is at once the source of supreme bliss and unparalleled satisfaction to the woman may become to her in effect the source of mental and physical anguish.

The anatomical construction of the female makes her desires differ from the masculine impulse.

The ultimate aim and object of desire is union of the male and female element, and to accomplish this in the natural way is to bring about the most complete physical coupling. Both parties have the same object in view, but the manner of its attainment depends upon the standpoint from which each proceeds.

The feminine instinct is directed toward the reception into the very center of its being and the retention there of the wherewithal to accomplish and fulfill its original design, and whatever energy is expended is to facilitate this process.

The physical mechanism that most effectively conduces to the consummation of the procedure is attended with local congestion and depletion which, in the case of the female, does not seem to involve the expenditure of quite as much energy as in the male.

It has been a matter of frequent observance that, other things being equal, women are capable of greater and more prolonged exercise in this capacity than are men, and, generally speaking, they do not reach the point of excessiveness as soon as do their consorts.

The matter of sexual excesses has been greatly overdrawn and after natural sexual relations have once become established and the novelty of the situation subsides, married women at least are very rarely injuriously affected by the frequency of natural sexual indulgences.

They are far more seriously and very much more frequently affected by abstinence from relations, suppression of desire and incomplete or improper performances than by natural intercourse, which is, beyond a doubt, more conducive to physical and mental well-being and attractiveness than the vast majority of people are aware.

The prevailing impression that men's ideal woman is without passion (though it may have a semblance of correctness in theory, is not so seriously taken in practice) makes women afraid and unwilling to admit their sexual inclinations, and leads them to suppress their desires. That some noble women at least, have strong sexual passions and suffer greatly by reason of their suppression is not sufficiently understood.

Aside from this there are other things which make women think themselves more frigid and with less sexual emotion than they really possess. Among these may be mentioned:

Disease or weakness of her sexual organs, especially after childbirth.

Fear of pregnancy and dread of the suffering and discomforts of childbearing, which are sometimes largely of their own making.

The trouble given by taking precautions to prevent conception and the uncertainty of the various methods employed acting as restraining influences on the ardor.

Ignorance of husbands about calling forth the desire and want of knowing how to do in order to effectively bring about the emotional climax.

Yielding to embraces without desire, together with giving evidence of performing a marital duty that is exacting and distasteful.

The tendency of women to want ruling and subjection by the man.

As a rule woman admires gallantry, but when it is carried to the point where she feels that her will is always the man's law, then her love is endangered.

Women admire not only the physical strength of men but their mental power as well, and since the psychic sphere is the greater in the woman, she can not, when she is conscious of her mental superiority, but feel a degradation when thusly associated that renders her feelings only lustful, or the play of the lower sexual centers.

It is unfortunate that the higher education of modern woman makes the choice of a desirable husband more difficult and the number of happy marriages less frequent, but in practice there seems to be a very perceptible tendency in this direction.

The prevalence of solitary sexual practices in women can not be given and only opinions can be stated, for no data upon this subject is available.

The term masturbation, as usually employed, conveys such a harsh meaning that when it is used in interrogating intelligent women, the reply is in nearly all instances a negative one.

When done by the male it is ordinarily only by means of some kind of friction upon the erectile organ itself, but the female may excite herself by manipulation of the clitoris, vagina, womb or breasts, and there are several methods by which it may be done.

The phenomenon may take place with very little active interference and by yielding to revery the impulse may be passively gratified.

Havelock Ellis thinks, "There can be no doubt that after adolescence, masturbation is more common in women than in men," and mentions an instance known to him in which "a married lady who is a leader in social purity movements and an enthusiast for sexual chastity, discovered through reading some pamphlet against solitary vice, that she had herself been practicing masturbation for years without knowing it. The profound anguish and hopeless despair of this woman in the face of what she believed to be the moral ruin of her whole life cannot well be described."

Such authors as Lawson, Tait, Spitzka, Dana, Moll, Rohleder, etc., believe that the practice is less common in women and girls than in the male sex.

Suduth, Kellogg, Berger, Cohn and others think it equally prevalent in both sex.

Among those who are of the opinion that women resort to solitary practices with greater frequency than men, may be mentioned Morris, Pouillet, Naecke, Moraglia and others.

It will thus be seen that no matter by what term it is designated and even though it be properly called a detestable vice, the practice is more or less generally shared by humanity.

Excitement has its charms and sexual excitement, whether recognized as such or not, is especially alluring and repeatedly sought by at least a majority of the people, without regard to sex, and who must be considered normal.

Among normal persons who have reached the age of discretion and who otherwise lead an exemplary and continent life, solitary sexual practices will hardly be sought, except for relief from existing conditions.

In women this most often happens about the time

of ovulation and whether purely mechanical or by the aid of imagination, it is not usually cultivated for pleasure or its own sake during the remainder of the lunar month.

CHAPTER IV

MALE SEXUAL SENSE.

What Constitutes a Normal Condition—If Purported Facts were True there would be Very Few, if Any, Normal Men—Boyish Habits—Sexual Knowledge Obtained from One who is Older in Experience—Females who Teach the Youth—Instinct and Curiosity Sufficient Causes for Erection and Sensation—Consciousness of Sex Acutely Enhanced by Puberty—The Youth Becomes a Man without Instruction and Does what His Father did—Characteristic Feature of Male Impulse is His Active Part in Matters of Sex—Gallantry and its Limitation—Codes of Social Law Expression of Man's Sexual Impulse—Seminal Emissions as Proof of Sexual Capacity—If Involuntary Emissions Always Indicate Disease, then Single Life is Abnormal—These Discharges Occur on an Average of 37 Times a Year—What Masturbation Means—Impossible for Boy to Grow to Manhood Without Artificial Acts—Emissions Without Intercourse Always Displeasing—Greatest Cause of Youthful Misery—Disgust Prevents Prolongation and Frequency of Habit—Masturbation Injurious when Excessive, with Bad Effects Functional and Transient.

Much has been written about sexual debility, perversion and pathological conditions affecting manhood, and very little attention has been given to the elucidation of what should be considered the normal condition of the masculine portion of humanity.

A thing is normal, or in its normal state, when strictly conformed to those principles of its constitution which makes it what it is, and abnormal when it departs from those principles.

Complete perfection is not to be looked for, and a normal man is one who conforms to the natural law or principles for which he was constituted or created.

To be a normal man does not mean to be of a certain height, weight, strength or mental caliber, but implies a condition which permits of the performance of those functions which are designated to, and are in compliance with, the natural order of his being.

To comply with these requirements he must be in both such a physical and mental state as will enable him to be adapted to his surroundings and live in accordance with social, as well as natural, laws.

The standard must vary with the conditions, for the abilities of a man at the age of sixty very greatly from those of the youth of sixteen, yet both should be considered normal.

The Esquimaux of the Arctics could not live properly with a tribe of negroes in interior Africa, while neither of these could conform to the exactions of the modern society of civilization.

It is difficult to formulate rules whereby to definitely measure the normal standard, and if one is to be governed by what appears in the daily press and elsewhere, or gives credence to what is commonly uttered in this relation, one would be forced to the conclusion that his own was an abnormal condition; but if he were possessed of proper knowledge and good judgment he would know that if the purported facts were true then there would be very few, if any, normal men.

With the donning of his first pair of knickerbockers, the little boy evinces a disposition to assert his masculinity, and any intimation that he is of the feminine gender is resented and his pugnacious spirit aroused.

As soon as he is able to willfully comply with the demands of nature unaided, he is constrained to seize the erectile member of the sexual organs in his hand and thereby facilitate the proper evacuation of the bladder. This invariably occurs each time he urinates and makes him familiar with the organ and accustomed to handling it.

Long before maturity, or the time when sexual excitement arises spontaneously, the boy will have become aware of the erectile property of his distinctive organ and the sensation accompanying this condition, because the local congestion which makes the erection is the result of some form of local irritation to which the boy is susceptible.

The condition of the prepuce, or foreskin, the fullness of the bladder, the irritation of climbing and the numerous other practices of the healthy, romping boy, to say nothing of the repeated retractions of the foreskin, which in the nature of things cannot be avoided, serve as sufficient causes for frequent erections.

If the irritations be sufficiently prolonged and of the nature to reflexly cause expulsive efforts, the mechanism and sensation of ejaculation will have been established and experienced before the time of the production of the vital fluid.

Probably everyone has their first actual sexual experience with an older person, or at least with one who has had some previous experience.

It is not at all rare for young boys to be initiated into the mysteries of sex by young women of much maturer years, who seek to satisfy their curiosity and passion by "playing" with boys, and thereby avoiding the possibilities of pregnancy and diminishing the chances of placing their reputation in jeopardy.

Outside of matrimony, a woman's first sexual experience is invariably termed "seduction," which implies the employment of subterfuge and force, but which in reality is simply a very important epoch in her career in which she took part, with some misgivings and reluctance no doubt, but also with a degree of willingness, if the act was successfully accomplished.

Men of good judgment and knowledge of the world and humanity can hardly expect an ordinary woman to acknowledge an illegitimate sexual intercourse, especially if it be her first, without having her stoutly maintain that she was forced into it, while the term "seduction" is not made applicable to the male.

It is the usual manner of expression, though hardly a correct statement of the actual facts, and should be taken very much as the common expressions of young women who assert they are "Just dying for a new dress," or "Would give anything to go to the show," and similar remarks which nobody is disposed to take literally.

The active part taken by women in real life, when it comes to the matter of love with a younger person, does not correspond to the conventional ideas.

Though nearly every woman receives her sexual initiation from a more experienced man, yet the number of youths who get sexual instruction and are taught what to do by females who are older—in experience at least—is certainly very large.

Probably a considerable proportion of middle class men can recall instances of their boyhood in which adolescent girls of the lower strata pursuaded them to acts of a sexual nature.

This common impulse which engenders curiosity—whether it be a seeking for information or a desire for sensation—is not confined to girls and women of the lower social order, though these are less frequently subjected to the restraints of self-respect and good breeding.

The active, playful boy is constantly seeking new methods of diversion, and in his anxiety to demonstrate and test his abilities he is continuously engaged in competitive sports and physical comparisons with his playmates.

It is but natural for this comparison to include the sexual organs and the little fellow would not be boyish if he did not make frequent attempts to test his expulsive powers and vie with his companions, when alone together, relative to the force and distance which the contents of the bladder could be propelled, and resort to whatever methods he could devise to facilitate this action.

These and many other practices that are essentially boyish lead to what will eventually produce a temporary distention of the spongy tissue in the pendant organ and cause erection, which is accompanied by a not unpleasant sensation.

Instinct, which Spencer defines as "compound reflex action," together with the inquisitiveness of childhood, are in themselves sufficient motives and causes for the boy to acquire a knowledge of the mechanism and sensation incident to sexual excitement.

One would be quite as successful in keeping a boy from scratching his head when it itched, as in preventing him at all times from retracting his foreskin.

Heredity no doubt greatly influences sexual precocity, and if the boy does not himself discover the manner in which voluptuousness may be excited, he will very probably, if associated with other boys, learn what induces eroticism.

When the sexual glands, or testicles, begin to develop and functionate, which occurs at puberty, the youth becomes more pronouncedly masculine, and thoughts centering about sexual matters come into the youthful mind with much greater frequency, and then there is in addition the internal messages which give rise to the impulse.

Careful teaching, good breeding and vigilance are great aids in facilitating subjection, but they are by no means sufficiently effective to suppress the sexual sense, for we now find consciousness of sex acutely enhanced.

Whoever asserts that boys grow to manhood without having had their sexual organs excited to activity, and without knowing that the sensations which accompany such excitations are due to their masculinity; is either misinformed, has but little knowledge of humanity, or deliberately mistakes or deviates from the truth.

To hold such a position is to maintain that the youth is without sex, for it is as natural for a healthy, robust youth to experience this mental and physical state, as it is for him to want to eat and play or have a desire to evacuate the contents of his bladder.

The evolution of modesty, which in the female is more pronounced, throws restrictions upon the male as well, and governs to a large extent his conduct and actions.

Without instruction and in spite of inhibiting influences, the youth spontaneously becomes a man and longs to do the things his father did before him, and which men will be impelled to do so long as there are men.

The most characteristic feature of the male sexual instinct is the active part which the man naturally assumes in matters sexual.

He is called upon to take the initiative and make the first move toward sexual union, and hence he is courageous, brave and more bold or daring than the apparently passive female.

He must gain the woman's favor and in many instances actively arouse her impulse, which he seeks to do by acts which inspire confidence, overcome modesty, insure protection and create admiration.

His early training and the society in which he moves determines his actions to a certain extent and governs his conduct, but in any event his aim is to establish himself in the good graces of a favored one of the opposite sex.

Next to his own preservation, he constantly seeks to guard the one whom his imagination conceives to conform to his requirements from the approaches of others, and to preserve her for himself. This solicitude, which is rooted in his own interests, begets his active attention and vigilance, stimulates his valor and often urges him to warfare.

The innate feminine coquetries, which are born of the mysteries of sex and are the result of the attractive being coupled with the repugnant, give an uncertainty that excites an eagerness to possess and calls forth gallantry and acts of devotion.

However liberal and generous a man may be, yet an extension of this generosity to the point of yielding to, or sharing with, another what he strives and longs for most, reaches the borderland of the superhuman and exacts that which manhood steadfastly rebels against.

The constitution of society has largely been in the hands of men, and the written and unwritten codes of social law are almost in their entirety the expression of man's sexual impulse.

By common consent the unpardonable sin is the violation of a law originating in sexuality.

When relief to the sexual secretory system is denied by nature's means, how shall the spontaneous discharges which relieve the system, after a certain degree of pressure or tension has been attained, be considered.

Strictly speaking, any seminal ejaculation that took place without actual sexual intercourse would be pathological, since it would not occur if the animal followed the strict law of its physical being without regard for its fellows.

When the sex glands begin to functionate, which marks puberty and which is long before the time when sexual relations are assumed, the vital fluid begins to be elaborated and secreted.

A pathological condition means an unnatural or a diseased state, and if we are to consider the process that is indicative of manhood and is a manifestation of masculinity and sexual capacity, as being an unnatural or diseased condition, then we should hold that the enforced restrictions of single life, or celibacy, are abnormal.

Nature has everywhere bountifully supplied the seed whereby the kind may be perpetuated and only an inconceivable small portion finds conditions favorable for its fructification.

The secretion of semen in the male, like ovulation in the female, is the natural or physiological process of adolescence and manhood, while its spontaneous excretion is evidence of the activity of the sex glands, and should—if we assume that the deprivation of sexual intercourse (which is nature's method of depletion) is at times natural and desirable—be considered as normal and physiological within certain limits.

These limits permit of great variation and depend largely upon the age, thoughts, associations, habits and actions of the individual.

The sexual glands are susceptible to the same influences as the mammary, lachrymal, salivary and other secretory glands of the body and their activity depends upon their blood supply, or stimulation.

Seminal emissions, except those occasioned by natural intercourse, are disgusting, and hence the cause of shame, and so knowledge of their occurrence is carefully guarded and kept secret.

The period of adolescence, or the decade between the ages of about 15 and 25 years, is a time of great bodily activity, with immature judgment and mentality, and as the majority of young men of to-day remain unmarried for the greater part of that time at least, they periodically experience a spontaneous evacuation of seminal fluid—if they live in strict chastity—which phenomenon is popularly designated as a "wet dream."

Many people with little common sense and less knowledge are prone to intimate that these discharges are abnormal and indicate a weakness or diseased condition, but if this were true then, indeed, would it be extremely difficult to find a healthy man.

With the view of demonstrating the existence of a sexual periodicity in the male, F. H. Perry-Coste, a recognized scientist, conducted a series of observations extending over a period of 13 years and found that spontaneous discharges occurred on an average of 37 times during a year.

These observations were made upon himself between the ages of 20 and 33 years and there seems to be no reason to doubt their accuracy, and so they might serve to form a fair criterion by which to judge at this age.

Owing to the many and varied influences which naturally tend to sexual excitement, this frequency might be given a considerable range of variation without giving rise to any marked degree of abnormality.

Aside from these involuntary emissions, the proper

study of the sexual sense demands the consideration of the willful or voluntary seminal discharges without the presence of the opposite sex in natural intercourse.

The consideration of homo-sexuality (by which is meant a feeling for a person of the same sex) and sexual perversion, which are both unnatural and abnormal, need not give us any concern.

There are extrinsic influences as well as intrinsic promptings which lead to seminal evacuations, and to which the youth is constantly susceptible.

The external influences which produce sexual excitement may cause the same, as has been previously stated, by impressions conveyed to the brain which call forth passion; or by local causes which produce turgescence, or erection—that is to say that the temporarily exalted sexual feeling, or passion, begins either centrally in the mind, or peripherally in the sexual organs.

The mental state is commonly the result of impressions by way of the special senses such as seeing, hearing or feeling a desirable person, which produce thoughts of a sexual nature.

The sight of statuary, a nude picture or glimpses of portions of a woman's body that are commonly concealed; the sound of a female voice or certain kinds of music, together with touching a beloved person often produces sexual excitement.

A distended bladder, inflammatory or other irritations of the pelvic organs, friction of the clothing and suggestive physical movements, as well as manual manipulations, cause erections which are accompanied by pleasurable sensations.

The temporarily increased local circulation being rythmical with general consciousness, and therefore pleasing, it is the natural inclination to prolong this pleasurable state, and if possible, increase it, until ejaculatory acts, or venereal orgasm, marks the height and termination of the sensation and transient physical condition.

Strictly speaking, masturbation means the employment of the hand to effect orgasm, but the term is generally extended to include any method by which this end is reached, except sexual intercourse.

If we consider every artificial means by which an orgasm is reached as being masturbation then it is extremely difficult to conceive how it is possible for a boy to grow into manhood without having this experience.

Voluptuous sensations have been observed very early in life—even in infancy, as the result of thigh rubbing—and normal persons recollect having these feelings from casual contact with the sexual organs at an early age.

In other instances there has been an occasional slight excitement from very early years, and there may be some cases in which there has been complete absence of sexual excitement until the age of puberty.

However pleasing the sensations which lead to ejaculation may be, and notwithstanding the frequency and tremendous force of the sexual promptings and youthful exuberance, yet these artificial emissions are, like the spontaneous discharges, regarded with displeasure and naturally evoke secrecy, shame and disgust.

Such discharges are also the source of the most formidable self-reproaches which manhood prompts.

The moral sense makes fear of detection dreadful, and the common belief in the injuriousness of the practice occasions the most horrible reflections in the mind of the growing youth, which tend to lessen somewhat the frequency of repetitions but which, powerful as they are, are yet inadequate to counteract the natural inclinations and permanently prevent recurrences during the earlier years of adolescence.

There is no one thing that causes the average boy in his teens so much misery and induces suffering from the pangs of conscience in his thoughtful moments, as the knowledge of his own solitary or artificial sexual practices.

Oftentimes these reproaches are prolonged into middle life and occasionally old men still attribute their ailments to what is termed youthful folly.

It is exceedingly hard to tell just how far admonition shall go, but it should not be carried to the point of so thoroughly frightening the youth as to destroy his morale and pluck. Nothing does this more readily than the false and fabulous stories which are told about the consequences of this habit.

Young lives are blighted and brilliant careers prevented by withholding the truth and grossly exaggerating or misstating the natural results of this habit.

Many men can look back upon their earlier lives and realize that the consequences of self-abuse were pictured to them in the most appalling colors and the efforts of their parents and teachers, with the kindest intentions, did more harm than good by their attempts to stop it. They subsequently, under conditions forgetting the past, find to their great astonishment that their powers are good and this proves to be their salvation. The knowledge of their retained manhood puts new life into them and convinces them that the statements of kindly disposed persons were erroneous, and they become sound men.

The very fact that artificial emissions are disgusting makes approaching manhood rebellious and prevents their frequency, while the increasing years bring added knowledge and maturer judgment.

Those whose nervous systems are naturally below par, or are already injured, most easily become habituated to this practice and indulge more immoderately than others, but the principle source of its evil is in the self-reproach and the struggle with the impulse.

When actual sexual experiences have been had, or normal relations have been established, these practices are usually discontinued, except perhaps in some instances, when they are resorted to in order to relieve a distressing tension which experience has proven may by this means be overcome.

The pulpit, the press, and medical literature as well, are wont to vividly depict most horrible results and ailments which are attributed to youthful sexual practices.

Insanity and scores of nervous and physical diseases are said to directly result from this sole cause.

No evidence can be produced to warrant such statements for though these conditions may be found in connection with such acts, yet where there is one case in which they occur, there are dozens of cases in which the practice has been quite as frequent and severe which present no permanently serious results, and, therefore, we must look for additional—not to say greater and more prolific—causes.

One has but to intimate to a credulous, and in this respect a simple young man, that he has committed such acts, and immediately he stand self-accused by his conscience and is convinced of his guilt, while the one who makes the charge runs no risk and, owing to the general prevalence of the practice during adolescence, can hardly be wrong.

Designing doctors and those who are sincere, but in this respect misguided, are responsible for immeasurable mental distress and suffering among young men, who are led to believe they are one among a very few who have indulged, and who do not know that the remainder of the sex has been subject to a similar experience.

If we look further for the causes of the general misconception of these facts, which society seems to entertain in this regard, we find that men are naturaly averse to frankly discussing this matter.

If an intelligent and gentlemanly fellow be interrogated regarding his own personal conduct in this respect, he will, if he does not resent it, be inclined to reply in a like manner as when asked if he has had "relations" with what was considered an estimable lady, and would, if he could not evade an answer, "perjure himself like a gentleman."

Public writers and speakers have generally ignored or not sufficiently considered, the influence of heredity and temperament when discussing sexual practices and have been disposed to treat the subject unscientifically and very much like the advocates of prohibition continue to consider the drink habit.

When describing the terrible results of alcoholic liquors these agitators fail to point out that the chief factor in cases of inebriety is not the drink itself but the person upon which the beverage acts.

Everyone who partakes of alcoholic drinks is by no means disastrously affected, and the majority of people of good parentage can bear witness that the moderate use of alcohol is not only consistent with good health, but even an occasional excess does not produce a lasting, serious result.

Regarding the habit of masturbation in adult life, Dr. Sturgis, who has had an extensive experience with venereal diseases in New York, considers: "Those who perform the act either while they are married or not, as not infrequently happens, as bachelors or as widowers, being restrained from seeking relief by illicit connection from a moral sense of wrong-doing or from fear of contracting a venereal disease. In these instances the bad results of the habit are much less noteworthy than they are where masturbation is indulged in during youth or early adult life; first, because the physical and mental conditions of the patient are much better calculated to withstand the effects of the habit, and secondly, because the subjects do not perform the habit so intemperately nor so frequently, indulging only so far as is necessary to relieve the urgent needs of their sexual organs. Such men usually masturbate no more frequently than they would practice sexual intercourse in ordinary married life. Under such conditions, the results, so far as my experience goes, seems to be but little, if at all, different from what they would be if coitus were indulged in. In this opinion I am aware that I am at variance with many of my colleagues who regard the effects of coitus and masturbation as not being identical. Act for act, I believe my position is correct; the danger in masturbation is the frequency with which the act can be performed in comparison with sexual congress; if a man could cohabit as frequently as he can masturbate the risk would be as great, because the nervous exhaustion would be as marked and as continuous, and that is the danger point in both cases. Another reason assigned for the difference in effects is the sense of shame attending masturbation which tends to depress the nervous system and injure the patient's morale. To a limited extent this is true; for, after coitus, the man is rather proud of his performance and glories in the sense of sexual power; but all masturbators are not by any means "broken up" by their habit. Some regard it as a choice between two evils, and while deploring the necessity, they think it a safer alternative than running the chance of contracting venereal disease. In this class of subjects, as well as in others that have been mentioned, much depends upon the natural physical condition of the patient; some men are naturally more vigorous, sexually speaking, than others, and are much better able to stand the reaction and slight exhaustion which follow even the normal performance of the sexual act, and in these cases it may be said that the habit produces very little if any bad results. While by no means apologizing for nor accusing indulgence in this evil habit, it may be said, taking into consideration the risk attendant upon intercourse with public women, and of the chances for contracting disease, that these patients perhaps pursue the wisest course, if it be positively necessary that they should indulge their sexual passions. This habit of masturbation, when it produces evil results, produces them for three reasons, one, because the physical condition of the patient is not sufficiently strong nor well enough established to resist and to overcome the nervous exhaustion which follows; two, because from the fatal facility with which the act may be performed, the continuous practice produces a continuous exhaustion and the victims have no time to rally between the performance of each individual act; and three, because the feeling of disgust and fright which has been induced in the patient by the lurid pictures drawn by well-meaning but injudicious friends and relatives tends to beget a nervous depression and hypochondria out of all proportion to the real injury done by the habit."

In writing a history of his own sexual experiences, an Australian who labors with the conviction that it is his life's mission to show others the sound way of living, says, with rare sincerity, after narrating the whole of his life: "A man like me has to go through a certain course of bad passions, restlessness, misery, gloom, and anxiety, till, if he is young, nature gradually heals him."

Honest judgment and frankness demand the statement that in healthy and well-born individuals, spontaneous and artificial seminal emissions, or simple masturbation, produce in themselves no bad physical results beyond some transient functional disturbances, and these are only considerable when the practice has been excessive.

We deplore the fact that we cannot consistently say something worse for a practice which is so nasty, disgusting and repulsive, but withal so general, and we hasten to dismiss the subject with alacrity.

CHAPTER V

THE COPULATIVE FUNCTION.

Sexual Conjunction the Natural Aim of Life—Pleasure the Incentive to Copulation—Hunger the Expression of the Nutritive Impulse, and Sexual Appetite the Result of the Reproductive Function—Satisfaction of Sense Immediate Object—Coitus a Process of Charging and Discharging—Intrinsic Influences Create Ideals—Extrinsic Causes make Emotion—Relief of Dual Exaltation Incidentally Perpetuates Race—Symptoms of Sexual Emotion—Vicarious Action of Bladder—Nervous Explosions—Giggling Girls—Exercise of Function Develops Character—Elevating Effect of Love—Suppression of Nature Leads to Abnormal Thoughts and Eccentricities—Mental Tranquility Incompatible with Physical Distress—Spontaneous Heightening of Female Feeling—Recurrent cycle of Male Physical Fitness Smaller—Coition Exacted—A Life Without Issue Cannot Reach its Highest Aim—Selfishness Most Prolific Cause of Misery but Parentage Transfers Center of Gravity to Another—Infant Begets Sympathy and Tenderness—Physical Affinity Between Mother and Child—Nursing and Copulation—Motherhood Brings Out Womanly Qualities—Innate Desire to Lavish Affection Upon Living Thing—Maternal Instinct—Conviction of Shortcoming Develops Dissatisfaction and Unrest—Physical Effects of Exercise of Function—Rotundity of Figure—Development of Female Bust—Proper Convexity a Great Charm—Intimate Relation with Vegetative Organs—Consistency Influenced by Sexual Organs—Exercise of Reproductive, Affects Capacity of Nutritive Function—Animal is Deprived of Gracefulness and Spirit by being Unsexed—Effects of Muscular Movement—Dancing as a Substitute for Copulation—Definition of Hysteria—Causation Attributed to Sexual Inactivity—Chlorosis and Hysteria a Show of Sexual Aptitude—Many Actions are Hypocritical and Hysterical—Insincerity where Copulative Function is Involved.

The creative power has endowed living things with the faculty of reproduction and has instilled into their being a desire to accomplish this end.

The pursuit of this aim must, in conformity with the ultimate objects to be attained, be prompted by an eagerness to fulfill its mission and be accompanied by a gratifying sense of pleasure. This inherent or fundamental characteristic of life is manifested by sexuality, or the sexual impulse, which forms the chief basis for the most massive of human emotions and the most brilliant of human aptitudes.

The natural aim of the sexual impulse is sexual conjunction, or copulation, which is the necessary act that precedes and leads to reproduction.

Conception, or the fusion of the male with the female element is itself insensible, but the act by which this fusion is made possible is naturally accompanied by the most profound sensations.

The essential physical qualification for sexual conjunction is distention, or vascular dilatation of erectile tissues, which means erection, or sexual excitement.

Pleasurable sensations are said to co-exist with vascular dilatation and low tension, while disagreeable senastions are apt to be accompanied by vascular constriction and high tension.

Practically the erectile tissue of the body is confined to the sexual centers, and since the tension is low here, when there is a temporary increase in the blood supply there is a pleasurable sensation, which accompanies the preparation for conjunction.

We have, then, in addition to the reproductive instinct, an immediate and most powerful incentive to copulation, which is—the most pleasurable of sensations.

Another great impulse which all life possesses is

that of nutrition, which is the only other impulse with which the sexual function can be compared.

Nutriment is necessary to prolong organic life, for if the energy expended by cellular activity is not replaced by food then there must be decay.

Life depends primarily upon the activity of the cells which compose its physical being, and as the human body is an aggregation of organs and tissues composed of cells dependent upon one another for sustenance and presided over by the mind, it follows that the combination of cells must have the same fundamental properties as the individual cell.

In order to have the cell obtain its required nourishment the food must be digested and assimilated, and so separate organs are provided for this purpose.

When the individual cells of the body desire food there is a general consciousness which we call hunger, or appetite, and which is referred to the receptive organ which is the natural avenue of supply—the stomach.

Digestion is normally insensible and, like conception, is made possible only after the ingestion of the wherewithal to accomplish its purpose.

The ultimate aim of eating and drinking is the nutrition of the body, but the immediate incentive is the satisfaction of hunger and thirst, which is gratified with the introduction of food and drink, though the process of assimilation requires a considerable period and the cells of the body do not actually receive the nutriment until some time afterward.

No one will presume to deny that there is pleasure in satisfying the sense of hunger.

Periodic recurrence of appetite is indicative of a healthy and normal condition.

The sense of taste was given us to discriminate between what is desirable and what is obnoxious.

The time, labor and energy expended in endeavoring to provide what gives the most pleasure while satisfying the demands of the nutritive impulse, occupies a very large part of our waking hours.

Human life may be indefinitely prolonged by partaking only of bread and water and the nutritive impulse thereby satisfied, but no civilized, healthy person thinks of restricting his or her diet to these narrow limits and everyone strives for what will give the most pleasure while gratifying the appetite for food.

The great incentive is the satisfaction of sense, with the attendant pleasures and subsequent feeling of well-being, be the ultimate object what it may.

The general consciousness manifested by hunger arises spontaneously, but the selective appetite for special things is acquired and developed by previous experience and knowledge.

Palatable dishes, stimulating drinks and the culinary arts are the result of a catering to agreeable sensations rather than the demands of nutrition, for humanity is prone to indulgences which are guided not so much by the bodily need as by the physical capacity for the time being.

This fact accounts for excesses in this respect, which are very numerous and oft-repeated, but which would never occur if there were any other incentive besides delightful sensations.

The reproductive function of the cell, in like manner as its nutritive property, finds an expression in individual sexuality, which is manifested by an appetite or sex hunger and which is naturally gratified by copulation, or union of the sexes.

Nature has provided special organs for the performance of this function, which act as agents for the combined cells that go to make up the body.

Just as the digestive system serves as an avenue for nutrition, so the generative organs are designed to perform the function of reproduction.

In the complex human organism, where all the parts are so closely interwoven and so highly special ized, no great manifestation can be confined to one single source, and though the sexual impulse is not the only root of the great human emotions, yet it largely enters into and molds these emotions and permeates the realms of love, sympathy, music, art and religion.

Owing to the intricate and many-fibred structure of the organism, the sexual impulse can be transferred into other channels and become a new force which is capable of strange and various uses, so that in the presence of all these manifestations we may say that this impulse everywhere plays a more or less conspicuous part in the production of the various human emotions.

The volcanic emotion engendered by the heightening of the sexual impulse is exploded and finds satisfaction in copulation, the preparation for and consummation of which is attended with the most intense and pleasurable sensations.

Like the pleasure given by the sense of taste incident to the partaking of palatable nourishment, so nature has made the sensations attending copulation the most enticing and satiating and given intense pleasure as the incentive to the performance of that function which must needs precede the perpetuation of the species.

The animal has no object in view when impelled to sexual congress save the one aim of expending the accumulated physical energy.

The function of copulation is a process whereby there is a charging and discharging of the nervous and sexual apparatus that is followed by deep organic relief.

The intrinsic or protoplasmic promptings are constantly and recurrently evolving what is manifested by sex, and the extrinsic influences, which association brings, cause ideals, images and desires to grow up in the mind, while at the same time the whole organism takes on additional energy and more than the usual amount of blood is to be found in the sexual apparatus. When this condition prevails the organism is in a state of sexual excitement, which demands a discharge of the congested sexual apparatus, together with a nervous explosion that relieves the tension and acts as an organic sedative.

The external influences which bring on the heightened desire, or passion, make the male more conspicuously active and serve the double purpose of bringing him to a state where discharge is urgent and imperative, and of causing an ardent emotional state in the female, together with a distention of her generative apparatus.

The direct incentive, desire or demand of this dual

exaltation, is the relief of the increased tension, which is effected by seeking a discharge of the sexual and nervous systems; and incidentally the act which must needs precede conception is accomplished, and indirectly that union which makes propagation of the race possible is effected.

The physiological emotion at time of the venereal orgasm is most powerful and overwhelming.

There is a volcanic motor and nervous explosion which reveberates through all the centers in the body, for the increasing tension becomes so great that the individual loses temporary control, and the ejaculatory acts are involuntary.

The physiological actions greatly simulate the symptoms of a mild form of epileptoid convulsions.

The circulation is increased with the rise of the emotion, the superficial capillaries are flushed, the face becomes reddened and the eyes brighten; a more or less profuse perspiration occurs over the entire body; there is increasing muscular activity, while the respiration is enhanced and the breathing becomes panting.

When the climax is reached there is a tonic muscular spasm throughout the body; the breath comes in gasps; the teeth are ground together (in some people there is a tendency to what is termed the "love-bite)" and the convulsive embrace, with an involuntary evacuation of the congested organs, terminates, with a deep sigh, in relaxation.

The turbulence occasioned by the orgasm is followed by a period of enforced repose, with the whole body tingling from the circulatory changes, and the reaction is one that induces sedation and balmy sleep.

Every bodily tissue has been in active participation, peristalsis has been active; the numerous sudoriferous and other glands have discharged their contents; waste products have been eliminated; there is a consciousness and satisfaction of having performed a vital fundamental function, and the mind is at ease while the body glows under the reaction.

It is difficult to conceive of another form of exercise which is so complete, and appetite again demands food and drink to complete the cycle.

In some respects emotion may be said to be "restricted motion," and Beaunis classes the sexual impulse with the "needs of activity."

Without motion there is no life, for death is the cessation of circulation. With increased circulation comes added warmth, and hence the frequent allusions to the heat of passion.

The circulatory changes are accompanied by mental unrest or agitation, which may be said to be a prompting to action or movement.

The increasing tension produces a corresponding degree of animation in which the instinctive desire is asserted and expressed by activity.

It appears that there is an intimate relation between the orgasm and the expulsion of the bladder contents.

The desire for urination frequently accompanies sexual emotion, especially in women, and the fullness of the bladder determines to some extent the sexual excitement.

Female animals make repeated attempts at urination during sexual excitement, and nocturnal seminal emissions are most apt to occur with a full bladder.

The nervous centers for micturition, erection and emission have been found to be in the lumbar enlargement of the spinal cord, and as the nerve supply is practically identical, the tension incident to emotion is more or less relieved by vicarious action.

Emotional states not infrequently find relief and burst forth in nervous explosions which produce convulsive laughing, and hence mirth and laughter are the usual accompaniments of sexual excitement, and spasmodic expiratory efforts not rarely precede or follow immediately after the climax of coitus.

The exuberance of adolescence is attested by boisterous demonstrations, and giggling girls become such upon the slightest provocation.

The exercise of the copulative function enters largely into the formation of the individual's disposition.

To deprive a being of ever yielding to its almost constant inclination is to impose restrictions that are truly exacting.

A character whose development is attained without the elevating effect of love can hardly be said to be broad and well poised, but is prone to be warped and tending to unbalance.

Pleasure is not confined to the gratification of the senses, but is a satisfaction of the mind as well, and it is difficult to conceive how one can be possessed of a contented mind and be satisfied with oneself when there is a consciousness of having suppressed or failed to comply with the dictates of its being, which finds an expression and satisfaction in sexual union.

Transgression of law is followed by pangs of conscience, for "to enjoy is to obey," not only social, but natural laws.

The conscious violation of social law brings remorse to people with self respect.

The prolonged suppression of the voice of nature which cries out for parentage and which is stilled by and demands the exercise of the copulative function, is not consistent with a desirable mind capable of proper reasoning, but leads to thoughts which deviate from the natural channel and enter pathways that traverse the labyrinth of a flighty, chimerical existence, and the result is prudery, eccentricity, misplaced sympathy and an imagination that departs from the normal and becomes deprecatingly fantastic.

Gastronomic abuses or disturbances are not compatible with an even temper and we are wont to ascribe irritability and "crankiness" to liver derangements, for if the nutritive impulse is not properly satisfied there is very apt to be a disturbed mental state.

It is useless to appeal to the judgment of a person who is starving without first supplying the bodily need, for the mind cannot be tranquil when there is physical distress.

The cravings of nature cannot be ignored indefinitely without affecting the mental equilibrium.

To be sure, the reproductive demands are not so frequent and imperative as the nutritive, but about thirteen times each year the female is unconsicously and involuntarily prepared for fertilization, which subconscious process cannot fail to affect the conscious mind, as the one merges into the other.

When the field that has been prepared is not fertilized by impregnation there can be no further growth, and nature casts off what now becomes useless.

The waste products, which are regarded, as is other decayed material, with disgust, appear in the menstrual flow and the field is cleared for another effort.

During the time when the soil is best fitted to accomplish its design there is a spontaneous heightening of sex feeling, which impels the woman to the copulative act, and this emotion is fully compensated in no other way.

During the progress of menstrual purgation or cleansing there is some disturbance of the nervous apparatus, and in women of refinement there is at least a consciousness of unfitness or inaptitude, and the discharge awakens revulsion.

Nature in its bounteous wisdom has made the male with a recurrent cycle of physical fitness that is smaller, which enables him to be adapted to conform to the female's readiness for fertilization.

Whatever the conditions or sensations may be that prompt a seminal emission, if it be not deposited within the female receptacle, the mental gratification will not be complete and manhood's desire will not be fully complied with.

That divine touch which gave the being animation exacts coition, and bestows therewith the greatest satisfaction, while it penalizes willful failure or omission with a troubled mind and accusing conscience.

Aside from the incentive of immediate pleasure, with temporary personal content, which the copulative function, when properly performed under suitable conditions, gives to its participants; there is an ultimate and remote but directly dependent state of mind which should be considered.

A life without issue cannot reach its highest aim and can hardly be said to have been well spent.

It is likely that the most prolific cause of misery is to be found in selfishness, but parentage, and especially the great principle of motherhood, is the transfer of the center of one's gravity from self to another.

After middle age we are impressed with the emptiness and futility of a life that is childless.

Woman, on whom the infant is naturally dependent for its sustenance and care, is the one more largely affected.

The helpless infant begets sympathy and tenderness, and not only the mother but the nurse to whom its care is delegated becomes strangely attached to her charge and keenly feels the effect of separation.

In the case of the mother suckling her child there is an additional physical affinity between the two which causes her thoughts and ideals to center about the little one who gives her pleasurable relief.

Nursing, or the passage of nourishment from mother to child, is a close physiological analogy to the relationship of a man and woman at the climax of the sexual act, and gives complete mutual satisfaction, both physical and mental, to mother and child.

Each needs the other for relief, and hence there is mutual desire, which is gratified with satisfaction.

The physical conditions correspond in that there is a bodily preparation which is manifested in distention of the glands of the breast by the accumulated secretion, which demands evacuation and which the necessities of the child require.

The mechanism is similar in that the introduction of the erectile nipple into the warm, moist and eager mouth of the infant causes spasmodic contractions and instinctive tugging at the erectile nipple, which calls forth the evacuation of the vital fluid that satisfies the infant's longing and brings to both a peaceful ease.

No one is at all times devoid of the yearning for offspring, and after all, when we have the necessaries of life, nothing really matters so much as the thoughts we think.

Ambitions, possessions or attainments do not fully compensate, for life can offer nothing satisfying in lieu of parentage, and especially motherhood.

Men's thoughts almost invariably change for the better with the advent of an heir, and many women who have been habitually absorbed in their dress, society or profession have become judiciously neglectful of these frivolities when brought to realize the joy and to experience the satisfaction of being a mother.

A willfully barren woman is usually the personification of selfishness and egotism, and neither merits nor receives the highest regard, but any woman, however foolish, has set her foot on the ascending ladder when she has ceased to be to herself the most important thing in her world.

This step is most effectively taken when she occupies her natural sphere and becomes a real mother—than which there can be nothing more ennobling and without which a contented or desirable mental state in her declining years is inconsistent.

A woman cannot be said to be really and truly a woman in all that the name implies until she has become a mother, for it is the state of motherhood that brings out the qualities that are so essentially womanly.

The realization of parentage leaves many contentedly silent upon its mellowing effects and the blissful consciousness of imparted individuality, while they are prone to dilate upon the added care and exacting responsibility; but childless men, as well as spinsters, eloquently voice most pathetically the incompleteness of an existence without posterity and often show their sincerity by lavishing their affections upon another's child, and not seldom upon living things that are not human.

Social conditions generally make young wives sensitive about assuming maternity immediately upon entering the marriage relation, and measures to frustrate this end are very often undertaken.

It is astonishing to note to what extremity women will go in their efforts to evade and overcome pregnancy, for the most absurd and often dangerous practices are restored to with the hope of postponing what they try to make themselves believe is for the time being an undesirable condition.

Sooner or later, however, the maternal instinct makes serious and throughtful ones realize the hollowness and unnatural state of such lives, and if they then find themselves incapable of becoming what they formerly strenuously resisted, they are truly to be pitied.

In this event when they become convinced of such inability, they are harassed by remorseful thoughts of previous conduct and are driven by the unstilled voice of their true inwardness to seek the physician's aid in their efforts to make amends.

The comparative freedom from responsibilities in their previous life, without the added cares of a family, has given them opportunities to cultivate their minds and æsthetic tastes, and we often find such women possessed of highly developed nervous systems and brilliant minds, which render them sensitive and susceptible beyond the ordinary.

The conviction of this personal shortcoming, which it is often found impossible to at all times successfully stifle, finds but partial atonement in professional, literary, charitable or social activities, while the nervous excitement which these engender makes the woman vulnerable, irritable and dissatisfied with these minor worldly blessings.

Nothing seems to give the relief sought for, and these cases tax the skill and ingenuity of the physician, who find their treatment difficult and numbered with the unsuccessful, while the patient may be considered fortunate if stimulants and narcotics are not resorted to and habitually taken.

The physical effect of the exercise of the copulative function is rarely sufficiently considered, nor are the bodily imperfections which may be attributed to its deprivation duly recognized.

The most attractive and prettiest—not to say the most beautiful—women of the world are to be found among those whose sexual relations are the least restricted.

The Parisians, whom the feminine world accepts as the leaders of fashion, have a reputation for gracefulness and vivacity, but they are also noted for their promiscuous love affairs.

It may be frequently observed that marriage brings to both men and women a rotundity of figure not hitherto possessed, whereas the word "spinster" awakens visions of a scrawny and angular physique.

The female bust has always been considered one of the great feminine charms and its development to a proper degree of convexity adds much to a woman's shapeliness.

The glands which make up this attractive frontal rotundity begin their development at the time of puberty, or when the other sexual organs take on additional growth, and their relationship with the pelvic vegetative organs is very close and intimate.

During menstruation there is often a greater tenderness or sensibility in the mammary region, and the changes which the breasts undergo with approaching motherhood are so distinctive that a first pregnancy can usually be detected by changes in the tissues about the nipples before the condition is positively manifested elsewhere.

It is reasonable to suppose that if menstruation

and the slight changes in the pelvic organs produced by the first few weeks following conception have their effect on the female bust, the exercise of the copulative function would also influence the consistency and contour of these frontal auxiliaries to female completeness.

Most women are solicitious and sensitive about the over or under development of their mammary possessions and not a few of them will even abbreviate the period of lactation, though it may prove detrimental to the child, when imbued with the idea of preserving a symmetrical figure, as there is a prevailing popular belief that the duties of maternity detract from physical shapeliness.

Other things being equal, the convexity and consistency of the feminine bust depends somewhat upon the exercise of the sexual organs.

The reproductive function is entwined with the nutrive, and exercise of the one affects the capacity of the other, and since copulation is the expression of this function, some of the trophic changes which are observed upon the establishment of sexual relations may be thus explained.

The intoxicating effects of stimulants are promptly relieved by coitus, and a greater amount of alcohol is tolerated by the system if coition is practiced about the time of its ingestion, as its force is expended in the energy involved.

The trite saying "The way to a man's heart is through his stomach," is but half the truth, as it applies only to nutrition and does not include the state of well-being which accompanies the increase of power that is vicariously utilized in the sexual capacity.

One effect of stimulating aliments is the accentuation of the twin impulse, for a mild intoxication prompts to acts of a sexual nature, and hence bacchanalian revelries go hand in hand with venery.

Physical gracefulness not only calls forth admiration but is itself produced by sexuality.

That the animal is deprived of spirit and animation by being unsexed is shown by the effect of emasculation in the stallion, who then no longer bows his graceful neck and proudly prances while he champs his bit with flaming eyes and widely open nostrils, but meekly trudges on his way with measured steps and gets but little notice.

The size and strength are but little affected by the inhibition of the copulative capacity, but the bodily posture with its symmetrical curves and graceful movements are greatly influenced by the copulative function.

Muscular movement is the most efficacious method of increasing muscular power—which means exhilaration—and the pleasure of witnessing movement becomes such by its stimulating effect on the muscular system.

Dancing is one of the highest forms of muscular movement and is the expression of joyous emotion. It not only acts as an excitant and is mildly intoxicating, but its effect on the spectator is pleasing, for the charm of the ballet would be greatly diminished if its personnel were not in motion.

The physical results of the dance are those of slight

intoxication—heightened color, brightness of eyes, graceful carriage and resolute air—and the mental effect is narcotizing and gratifying.

In the pleasure and relief that it gives, dancing very often acts as a substitute for the natural gratification of the sexual impulse, and young women who find themselves unequal to other exertions frequently expend a vast amount of energy at a dance without becoming fatigued, but are thereby relieved and gratified.

It is noteworthy and significant that after marriage, with the exercise of the copulative function, girls generally lose much of their ardor in dancing.

Since the time of the ancient Greeks a number of vague nervous manifestations have been observed for which an adequate pathological condition cannot be demonstrated.

It was believed that this condition was due to the womb, and it was therefore called hysteria.

Hippocrates described hysteria as "suffocation of the womb," and Plato states that "In men the organ of generation—becoming rebellious and masterful, like an animal disobedient to reason, and maddened with the sting of lust—seeks to gain absolute sway; and the same is the case with the so-called womb, or uterus, of women; the animal within them is desirous of procreating children and, when remaining unfruitful long beyond its proper time, gets discontented and angry, and wandering in every direction through the body, closes up the passages of the breath and, by obstructing respiration, drives them to extremity, causing all varieties of diseases."

It is, of course, impossible to maintain this theory in its crude form in modern times, but the fact remains that the causation of hysteria is still difficult to satisfactorily explain at all times, and there seems to be a tendency to disregard the sexual factor and ignore the copulative function in the consideration of this affection.

Freud, of Vienna, who began as a disciple of Charcot, after recent extensive investigations upon hysteria, says: "The weightiest fact on which we strike in a thorough pursuit of the analysis is this: From whatever side and from whatever symptoms we start, we always unfailingly reach the region of the sexual life. Here, first of all, an etiological condition of hysterical states is revealed."

Ellis observes: "The sexual orgasm has this correspondence with the hysterical fit, that they both serve to discharge the nervous centers and relieve emotional tension."

Chlorosis, which is found in young women with poor blood, is often associated with hysteria and most frequently occurs in remarkably pretty girls who have had no sexual experience but who possess all the sexual and reproductive aptitudes which make women attractive to men, and Ellis states that "Chlorosis is a physical phenomenon, hysteria an auto-erotic psychic phenomenon; yet both alike may be regarded to some extent at least, as sexual aptitude showing itself in extreme and pathological forms."

That many, very many of the actions of the people in modern society are hypocritical and hysterical one can scarcely gainsay, and education has made conversation capable of disguising the innermost thoughts.

Except on rare occasions, people can act and fluently say the things they do not really feel.

Insincerity has become a striking characteristic, and this is most noteworthy, though in a certain sense, it may be, pardonable, in the many instances in which there is an involvement of the copulative function.

CHAPTER VI

THE ACT OF COPULATION.

Human Nature the Most Important Fact—Cases of Unsatisfactory Sexual Life Numerous—Essential Requisite is Mutuality—Orgasm the Aim and End, and Act should be Preceded by Abbreviated Courtship—Physiology of Act—Mechanism in Male and Requirements for Fitness—Timely Orgasm with Semen Deposited within Vagina Necessary for Satisfaction—Source of Either Woman's Pleasure or Anguish—Always Pleasurable when Rightly Done—How Orgasm in Woman is Produced—Action of Womb During Climax—Nervous Tension Relieved by Act—Nervousness Always Accompanies Disturbance of Sexual Function—Sympathetic Nerve Connection Between Pelvic and Abdominal Organs—Dyspepsia and Vomiting of Pregnancy Arise from Uterine Congestion—Mechanism of Digestion—Nervi Erigentes the Direct Connection Between Brain and Genitals—The Physical Linked to the Mental Being by Vaso-Motor Nerves—How Mental and Sexual Functions Affect Each Other.

A goodly proportion of the people in civilized countries are little better off than savages in some respects.

This is made evident by their foolish superstitions, their unnatural habits and their indifference to the sufferings of others.

One of the chief, if not the greatest, causes of this condition is to be found in the fact that we have not yet changed our system of education so as to include all those things which go to make up a normal, and therefore desirable, existence capable of the greatest good.

It is not only possible for young people to go through a public school, high school and college and come out without a knowledge of the most important truths of life, but it is very probable that they do, and in addition they are trained to be prejudiced against those who are teaching the real facts about man and the universe.

Thousands of men in every civilized country get their living by teaching old ideas which have been found out to be wrong, and many gain fame and pecuniary benefits by expounding theories that have long since been exploded.

If a young man wishes to become an electrician or an engineer he is taught the latest and most complete knowledge that the world possesses, but if he is to be a minister, lawyer or doctor he is required to memorize a lot of statements from musty old books written by men who never saw electric light, except in a thunder storm, and who never crossed a bridge made of iron or rode in a railway train.

The most important fact in the world is human nature, yet how few of us know how it has been developed, and how many are given an opportunity to correctly study it.

We do not know how man got his body or where his mind came from, nor can we explain conception any more than we can tell how the grass which makes the fields green, grows.

We do know, however, that there is such a thing as

growth and that some circumstances favor it and other conditions prevent it.

We know, too, that adult human beings are impelled to copulate, and observation has taught some of us that this impulse actuates many of our motives and influences our well-being, yet ordinary persons are left to blindly grope in darkness when it comes to acquiring knowledge about how best to meet this requirement, and in this respect they are no more intelligent than the people who lived hundreds of years ago, and are seemingly content with the superstitions and theories of ancient ancestors, which have in nearly every other respect been proven to be fallacious and crude.

In the learned professions there is a tendency to regard the oldest ideas as the best ones, for all new ideas are considered as dangerous, and any attempt at the ventilation of ideas or demonstration of facts concerning the sexual relation is met with derision, skepticism and rebuke.

A thorough analysis of the sexual act is made difficult by reason of its sacredness or unspeakableness, and little more than bare mention of its occurrence is to be found, but so long as ignorance is deemed preferable to enlightenment, so long will misery prevail where happiness and comfort could readily be had if information were obtainable and reason and common sense employed.

That the sexual act is very much more frequently disappointing than mutually gratifying is painfully evident, and even those who express a conviction that their relations are all that can be hoped for, will, in a burst of confidence to one whom they believe to be worthy and well qualified to advise, disclose circumstances which, if they were not so tragical and disastrous, would be appalingly ridiculous.

It marriage means anything, it signifies not only a willingness, but implies an anxiety to assume the sexual relation, with its concomitant pleasures and ultimate results.

To be repeatedly told by intelligent and, in other matters, well informed persons that there is no more pleasure and far less satisfaction to be derived from the sexual act than is experienced by mere social intercourse, is to be convinced that the guidance of individual instinct alone, which is greatly modified, not to say perverted, by education and social conventions, is not prolific of those relations which are necessary to mental and physical well-being.

Copulation, coition, sexual congress, conjunction or embrace, are terms used to designate the union of the sexes in the act of generation.

This involves the closest possible physical juxtaposition, after suitable preparation, and entails the expenditure of more or less energy and effort.

When we consider the motives which occasion the act, we are convinced that the chief characteristic and essential requisite to its proper fulfillment is—MUTUALITY.

Any other condition except the one in which both parties are simultaneously actuated by the desire to both give and take delight, can not bring to either all that this function affords.

Cheerful acquiesence and eager participation in

its consummation are necessary for subsequent mental tranquillity and satisfaction, be the other conditions and results what they may, and this is attained only with temporary physical fitness.

Courtship, or soliciting favor by obliging compliance with the wishes of another, is the preparation of the sexes for union, and, in order to be effective, every act of copulation should be undertaken with an abbreviated courtship.

The aim, end and climax of copulation is orgasm, by which there is an involuntary depletion of the temporarily congested sexual organs.

Complete and normal copulation is physiologically both voluntary and involuntary in either sex, and, for convenience of description, may be divided into three stages.

The first or preliminary stage is wholly and completely under the control of the will, and consists in the preparation or charging of the system for the discharging process, or orgasm.

Under suitable conditions and surroundings, the solicitation of favor is manifested by a mutual interchange of gentle caresses, which gradually merge into suggestive acts that are reciprocal and progressive, and which elicit delightful anticipatory subjective sensations.

With physical coupling and gradually increasing simultaneous undulations, the nervous sensations are increased and intensified to a height where mental control is no longer possible, and involuntary acts ensue in which every portion of the being seems to take an active part, and by which the sexual apparatus is depleted and the nervous tension relieved.

The subjective sensations accompanying these involuntary actions it is impossible to adequately describe as there are no feelings akin to them and nothing known to humankind is comparable therewith.

Suffice it to say that there is the greatest possible emotion, which occasions convulsive muscular agitation, and a sort of scattering or explosion that is profoundly reactive.

The final stage is one of delightful relaxation with a sense of comfort and well-being, and a tendency to sweet repose, which is followed by a mental attitude that secretly cherishes a sacred memory of the circumstance, entertains the kindliest feelings toward the party and subsequently seeks a repetition with impatience.

In our monogamous life it is impossible to separate the act from the actor, for recurrent memory always associates the two, and hence the strongest of human ties are thus securely cemented.

The first requisite for normal copulation, so far as the male is concerned, is a sufficiently vigorous erection of the virile member to permit of intromission.

This is accomplished by a temporary increase in the blood supply, which fills and distends the spongy tissue in the organ and renders it hot and rigid.

Coincident with this distention and consequent erection of the copulative member, the entire sexual organs are congested and become functionally active.

The friction occasioned by the undulations, reflexly causes the expulsion of the contents of the vasa deferentia, the seminal vesicles and the prostrate, which secretions commingle, and when this fluid reaches the posterior urethra its ejaculation is facilitated by the spasmodic and synchronous contractions of the sphincter ani, levator ani, ischii and bulbo-cavernosi muscles, together with the muscular fibres of the urethra.

This action causes the seminal fluid to be emitted in jets with profound constitutional emotion.

The intensity of emotion differs greatly in individuals and at different times in the same individual, owing doubtless to the difference in temperament and the condition of the pelvic organs.

Usually after a period of continence, when the seminal glands and receptacles are more or less filled with the fluid, it requires comparatively little friction to induce emission; whereas, if the evacuation has taken place a short time previously, a more vigorous and prolonged period of copulative activity is tolerated and required for orgasm.

It is not enough for the male to have the physical qualifications for the act if normal results are to be obtained.

The full physiological and beneficial effects of copulation are obtained only by the proper performance of the act.

The sexual act is very much like any other physical action, such as walking, running, dancing, swimming, etc., and a proficiency in its accomplishment is acquired in very much the same manner.

To be sure, there is an instinctive prompting to action, but the required co-ordination of movement must be obtained by individual experience.

Any person who is suddenly precipitated into deep water will instinctively go through a series of muscular movements, and if he has learned how to swim these movements will be co-ordinate and rythmical and not only keep him afloat but enable him to propel himself; whereas, if he has had no experience in the water the movements will be irregular and consequently ineffective.

Most anyone who is normally constituted can learn how to swim, but they must go into the water, persist in their efforts and have confidence in their ability.

Though they must learn for themselves, and would probably do so if they did not become discouraged, yet instruction greatly facilitates their progress and encouragement begets self-confidence.

Copulation is in some respects like swimming, and though most men eventually learn to accomplish it after a fashion, yet comparatively few become quite proficient.

The two may further be likened in that the educational and social attitude is such that married people, and especially those about to be married, are too often cautioned that, to avoid disaster, they should "deny themselves" in their natural indulgences, which has about the same effect as the admonition of the fond mother who seeks to guard her children from a watery grave by granting them permission to enjoy the delights and benefits of bathing with the injunction to "Hang your clothes on a hickory limb, but don't go near the water."

In either event, if the advice were heeded they

would be but poorly equipped to battle with the "tempestuous seas" which inevitably break, sooner or later, upon the shores of their future life.

Luckily for the child such a rule is more often "honored in its breach than its observance," but the man too often seeks to conserve his power by abstaining from that which, if practiced, would only make him the more masterful.

There is but one finish to proper copulation, and that is—simultaneous orgasm, with ejaculation into the upper extremity of the vaginal passage.

Anything short of this does not completely suffice for the satisfaction of the natural sexual instinct.

Time is the essence of this, as well as other contracts, for an untimely orgasm is invariably disappointing and unsatisfactory.

It is almost normally the function of the male to arouse the female, and since mutuality is the essential requisite for satisfactory coitus, it behooves the male to so conduct himself as to bring about this condition at the proper time.

When a woman manifests a persistent indifference in sexual relations and fails to obtain gratification, we should remember that the fault may not be due to herself alone, but in part at least to a husband who does not know what is required and fails to successfully play his part.

Women may never experience the gratification and relief of intercourse and become sexually frigid through the ignorance of the husband who, however, kindly disposed, does not know how to proceed.

The shock and suffering indured by the young

wife in the nuptial bed is too frequently prolonged into after-life and may seriously mar the connubial bliss.

For the husband there must be some slight degree of pleasure in coitus or it can not take place at all, but the wife may lend herself to the act without any pleasurable participation, for to her what under some conditions, in the emotions which it arouses and the gratification it brings, will cause everything else to dwindle into insignificance, will under other circumstances be the source of torture.

The belief that a woman has nothing to get ready for intercourse is pretty generally prevalent, and to this erroneous impression may, in a measure, be attributed a large part of the existing domestic discord.

Copulation can not be complete without orgasm, and it is impossible to produce an orgasm without congestion of the sexual apparatus, for there can be no discharging when there has been no previous charging.

Though the man's pleasurable excitement is necessary for the woman's sexual gratification, yet the reverse is not the case, as the woman will have no orgasm without previous desire, and if this be lacking, copulation for the man will be but partially satisfying.

Pleasurable sensation being the immediate object of copulation, it remains, then, to consider what conditions will best contribute to that mutuality in which is found the greatest happiness and without which no life is complete and no normal person content.

There is perhaps no person who is at all times wholly indifferent to the good will and caresses of another. The man or woman who is kissed by a desirable person of the opposite sex feels a satisfying sense of pride and is thereby elated and moved to reciprocate.

A manifestation of reciprocity, wherein lies the charm of affection, begets a desire to please, inspires confidence and invites repetition and progression, which are necessary auxiliaries to the preparation for union.

The desire is instilled by nature, which awakens imagination and creates ideals, and there usually appears, sooner or later, in nearly every career some person who, in a measure at least, fits this created image and the association of ideas makes this person the embodiment of the strongest desires.

The promptings and joyful expectations come from within, but the realization of the hopes depends, to a great extent, upon the conduct of the persons involved.

If disappointing results are to be avoided there must be not only proper but timely conduct in the presence of the right and fit person.

That is to say, certain personal actions must be undertaken, and these acts must occur at such a time as the occasion demands, but at such a time only, for if they be premature or belated they become disgusting and intolerable.

The greatest kindness that can be shown a person whose physical condition is such that sleep is imperative and rest urgently demanded, is to allow him or her to remain unmolested and enjoy what is for the time being most needed for a state of well-being, and caresses at such a time, even when coming from a most devoted person are not only received with indifference, but actually become irksome and intolerable.

When suggestive actions do not elicit response they have a tendency to create anger and resentment.

The same overtures which from one person, at a proper time and under suitable conditions, are highly flattering and considered as the greatest honor, will from others and amidst inappropriate circumstances, merit the sternest rebuke and be construed as the basest insult.

In injudicious acts may be found a prolific reason why "Heaven knows no rage like love to hatred turned," and those crimes which are considered the most heinous and are by common consent the most abhorrent, are those irregular, inappropriate and diabolical attacks prompted by selfish passion and directed to the forcible violation of the inalienable right to individual sexual preference and willingness.

The brutality of such acts when committed upon a female other than the one with whom the marital relation is recognized, appeals so strongly to the common mind that the civil law designates them as rape and severely punishes the transgressors.

But what shall be said of the relation between husband and wife in which, though there be no great physical violence or actual bodily injury perpetrated, yet in which the mental anguish caused by enforced submission without desire occasions quite as severe suffering as bodily wounds?

As an instance of one out of many thousands of cases in which great misery is the direct result of ignorance of human nature and want of the knowledge which is necessary for the creation of the essential conditions for the copulative act, the following communication may be cited as fairly typical:

"Is it possible for a woman who is absolutely devoid of the sex nature so to cultivate the same that the marital obligation will not be a torture to her? I am very healthy, in fact, my health is far above the average and always has been. I am thirty years old and have been married four years. My life so far has been more than an ordinarily happy one, but within the past year I have felt sometimes that my husband was in some way growing apart from me, and after much thought I have reached the conclusion that the growing estrangement is owing to the fact that I cannot respond as a wife should. My husband is a strong, healthy, vigorous man in the prime of manhood—thirty-six—and with all of a strong man's ardent, passionate nature. He is never unreasonable, never brutal, and yet I submit to his wishes with such a loathing that I fairly hate myself for it. I know in my heart that the time will come when I shall lose his love, and I shall owe it to the fact that I was born a stone, instead of a flesh and blood woman. Oh! if you can only suggest something, if you can tell me how to avert this impending wreck of my life, there is nothing I can write that will express my gratitude. This is probably the first time that you have ever had such a request, but I believe you are broad enough to respect any question asked in sincerity, and I feel that you will appreciate the fact that it is a cry for help from one who is suffering mental agony."

In all probaility this is one of the numerous cases of unequalized sexuality in which two mature people in the prime of life and vigorous health do not "come together" as they should, and in consequence their lives are embittered, as the greatest pleasure that life affords is denied them.

The woman, by submitting without desire and the attendant physical fitness, becomes disgusted with herself and in addition fails to satisfy her husband.

The woman's desire needs to be actively aroused, for a state of physical fitness must needs be followed by a mental inclination, and then her condition of passivity naturally passes into that of active and eager participation.

It is the province of the husband to bring about this required bodily condition, and if he is unable by himself to do so, it can be readily accomplished by the aid of local applications to the genitalia, which produce a temporary turgescence, or the required physical condition.

In some cases greatly delayed normal sexual relations, when the impulse is not altogether latent, tend to induce all manner of perverted and abnormal sexual gratification as a substitute for natural copulation, for the sexual apparatus in woman is very complex and has difficulty in responding to sexual excitement with which it is not familiar.

It has been said that "love begets love," and this is quite as true of sexual desire as of Platonic affection.

It is eminently fitting and natural to "welcome the warm approach of sweet desire," and the smouldering embers of sexuality are enlivened by the gentle carasses of a desirable person, which kindle and feed the flame of a burning passion or desire to possess; or they are smothered and extinguished by a sudden precipitation of the ashes of a prematurely consuming conflagration.

Not every woman is like Pope's "Wife of Bath," who was blessed with a "wondrous gift to quench a flame," but almost any healthy woman can, by proper treatment, be aroused from a sexual lethargy and imbued with an overwhelming desire to enjoy, and the man who succeeds in effectively bringing about this condition to the exclusion of others, is assured of subsequent remembrance and favor.

Erection of the copulative organ in the male is accompanied by sexual excitement, and in like manner, distention of the female erectile tissues produces sexual desire.

Instead of having the erectile tissue confined to one organ, as in the male we find it more widely distributed in the female.

The clitoris which is analogous to the penis of the male is composed of erectile tissue and its object is to furnish to the female the nervous erethism which is necessary to a perfect performance and completion of the sexual act.

In fact it may be said to be the organ of voluptuousness in the female by the excitement of which outside of the sexual act an orgasm and ejaculation of mucus from the Bartholinian glands is produced. (Munde Dis. of Women.)

The nymphae or inner lips of the vulva also contain erectile tissue, and the same is found in the vagina, the urethra and the vestibule.

The filling and distention of this tissue with blood brings to the parts added heat and moisture, and occasions sexual excitement.

A very liberal distribution of the terminal filaments of sensitive nerves to the clitoris and lower portion of the vagina, gives to these parts added sensibility and makes them the points of greatest sensitiveness.

Unlike the male, who, under sexual excitement, is actuated and impelled to the deepest possible penetration; the female is imbued with a desire to incorporate to the full limit of her receptive capacity; and the repeated attempts and exertions made to accomplish this purpose bring pressure and friction upon the most sensitive areas, which produces an intensity of feeling that reflexly calls forth involuntary spasmodic muscular action, or orgasm.

The voluntary muscles directly concerned in the orgasm are those whose union takes place at the perineum, or the space between the anus and vulva.

The contraction of this group of muscles throws the perineal body forward and upward, forcing it toward the anterior wall of the vagina and at the same time compressing the vulvo-vaginal, or Bartholinian glands, which causes the secretion of these glands to be emitted in jets.

In some cases of irritation this action is so strong as to become abnormal and to cause dyspareunia, or to render coition entirely impracticable.

In addition to the spasmodic contraction of this group of voluntary muscles at the climax of the sexual act, there is spasmodic contraction of the involuntary muscular fibres which go to make up the internal organs of generation, and a consequent out-pouring of the glands contained in the tract.

That there is spasmodic action of the vagina is very probable and that there is uterine activity during the orgasm there can be little doubt. A rythmical contraction and dilotation of the cervix has been frequently observed.

Dr. Munde in Amer. Jour. of Obstetrics, vol. XVI p 846, says: "We ourselves have seen the gushing, almost in jets, of clear, viscid mucus from the external os, during evident sexual excitement, produced by a rather prolonged digital and specular examination in an erotic woman. The lips of the external os alternately opened and closed, with each gaping emitting clear mucus, until the excitement, which we confess to having intentionally prolonged by gently titillating the cervix with a sound through the Sims' speculum; reached such a height as to cause the woman to sit up on the table and thus end the experiment."

In commenting upon the foregoing, Dr. Upshur in "Disorders of Menstruation," states: "I myself have seen the same condition of things occur more than once. The fact is this: Under the stimulus of sexual excitement, the cervix becomes engorged with blood and softer, the os expands, and the canal of the cervix dilates so that a sound, which could not pass through the cavity before, is easily admitted now; at the same time the cervix is thrust forward and there is a gaping, suction action by which the seminal fluid is sucked into the canal of the cervix. So soon as the orgasm ends, it returns to its normal condition."

That there is uterine activity during an orgasm may be demonstrated by the employment of one of those so-called "womb supporters" which are in common use.

If one of these soft rubber pessaries or caps be adjusted over the cervix and allowed to remain during an orgasm, it will be found, upon subsequent removal, to contain a considerable amount of fluid that has come from the interior of the womb and which would not be found in the usual quiescent state of this organ.

It has also been noticed that orgasm, and especially repeated or prolonged and ardent sexual intercourse, about the time of expected menstruation, has a tendency to bring about and increase the usual menstrual flow, and it may be that in this action of the womb at the copulative climax is to be found one reason why prostitutes, or those women who persistently and ardently worship at the shrine of Venus, become pregnant with comparative rarity.

The histories of many women confirm the belief that there is increased sexual desire, exclusive of extrinsic influences, in that third of the month during which menstruation appears, and this is undoubtedly due to the hyperæmic condition of the internal generative organs at this time.

Most women are warned of the approach of the menstrual flow by some nervous disturbance, for just before and at the time of the normal menstrual period, there exists a certain amount of vascular and nervous tension throughout the body, which manifests itself by a tenderness and fullness of the breasts, with certain feelings of malaise, nervous excitability, etc.

After menstruation and the subsidence of the hyperæmic condition of the pelvic organs there is cessation of the nervous tension.

During sexual excitement, when there is distension of the erectile tissues, there is also a congested condition of the pelvic organs, together with more or less great constitutional tension, or emotion, which is relieved by the orgasm, after which a condition of pleasing relaxation ensues.

If, for any reason, there be failure of orgasm, with its relief of temporary tension, there will remain some slight degree of disturbance.

Oft-repeated sexual excitability without orgasm, extending over a long period, will eventually cause an instability in the nervous mechanism, and, therefore, the author is inclined to agree with those who believe that there is a far greater number of modern women, who would be otherwise healthy, but who suffer from deprivation of physiological copulation; than those whose ailments have been attributed to so-called excessive indulgences.

Many, very many, nervous women who find but little real pleasure in life, would be greatly benefited by natural intercourse at regular intervals.

The narrative of an intelligent English lady with extraordinary judgment, keen observation and unusual frankness, tells of her engagement and the earlier part of her married life, and so well illustrates this point that it is given in her own words, which are as follows:

"There was considerable difficulty in the way of marriage, but we saw a good deal of each other. My fiance often dined with us, and we met every day. The result of seeing him so frequently was that I was kept in a constant state of strong, but suppressed, sexual excitement. This was particularly the case when we met in the evening and wandered about the moonlit garden together. When this had gone on about three months I began to experience a sense of discomfort after each of his visits. The abdomen seemed to swell with a feeling of fullness and congestation; but, though these sensations were closely connected with the physical excitement, they were not sufficiently painful to cause me any alarm or make me endeavor to avoid their pleasurable cause. The symptoms got worse, however, and no longer passed off quickly as at first. The swelling increased; considerable pain and a dragged-down sensation resulted the moment I tried to walk even a short distance. I was troubled with constant indigestion, weight in the chest, pain in the head and eyes, and continual slight diarrhœa. This went on for about nine months and then my fiance was called away from the neighborhood. After his departure I got a trifle better, but the symptoms remained, though in less acute form. A few months later the engagement was broken off, and for some weeks I was severely ill with influenza and was on my back for several weeks. When I could get about a little, though very weak, all the swelling was gone, but pain returned whenever I tried to walk or stand for long. The indigestion and diarrhœa were also very troublesome.

I was treated for both by a physician, but without success. Next year I became engaged to my husband and was shortly after married. The indigestion and diarrhœa disappeared soon after. The pain and dragging feeling in the abdomen bothered me much in walking or any kind of exercise. One day I came across a medical work in which I found description of symptoms like those I suffered from, ascribed to uterine disease. I again applied to a doctor, telling him I thought there was displacement and possibly congestion. He confirmed my opinion and told me to wear a pessary. He ascribed the displacement to the relaxing climate, and said he did not think I should ever get quite right again. After the pessary had been placed in position every trace of pain, etc., left me. A year later I thought I would try and do without a pessary, and to my great satisfaction none of the old traits came back after its removal, in spite of much trouble, anxiety, sick nursing and fatigue. I attribute the disorder entirely to violent sexual excitement which was not permitted its natural gratification and relief. I have reason to believe that suppression acts very injuriously on a woman's mental capacity. When excitement is naturally relieved the mind turns of its own accord to another subject, but when suppressed it is unable to do this. Personally, in the latter event, I find the greatest difficulty in concentrating my thoughts, and mental effort becomes painful. Other women have complained to me of the same difficulty. I have tried mechanical mental work, such as solving arithmetical or algebraic problems, but it does no good; in fact, it seems only to increase the excitement. (I may remark here that my feelings are always very strong, not only before and after the monthly period, but also during the time itself; very unfortunately, as, of course, they cannot then be gratified. This only applies to desires from within, as I am strongly susceptible to influences from without at any time). There seems nothing to be done but to bow to the storm till it passes over. Anything I do during the time it lasts, even household work, is badly done. The brain seems to be addled for the time being, while after gratification of desire it seems to attain an additional quickness and cleverness. Perhaps this cause contributes to the small amount of intellectual and artistic work done by women, admitting their natural inferiority to men in artistic impulse. A woman whose passions are satisfied generally has her strength sapped by maternity, while her attention is drawn from abstract ideas to her children."

We are, all of us, very prone to recognize only objective acts, and too frequently fail to take cognizance of, and are blind to, subjective symptoms and sensations.

A congested condition of the generative organs causes emotion (which may be said to be restricted motion) restlessness, nervousness and excitability; while a depletion of the same relieves the tension, restores an equalized circulation and brings about a calm and tranquil ease.

In the male, where the physical manifestations of congestion are largely external, they are very readily recognized, and the subjective sensations occasioned by this condition are easily associated with their cause.

In congestion or inflammation of the male sexual apparatus, such as is generally caused by gonorrhœal infection, we usually find, among others, the following symptoms:

Sexual ardor easily aroused, even by anything the least suggestive; emissions premature during coitus and devoid of the normal amount of satisfaction; pollutions frequent and followed by a feeling of weakness and depression; nervous phenomena of a subjective type and varying according to the temperament of the patient, but always suggestive of neurasthenia, though not of any particular variety; later, when the condition becomes chronic and prolonged, the excitability gives way to depression, when the erections and emissions become less frequent, sexual desire gradually disappearing, and indifference to female society supervening, with the external genitals becoming relaxed, anæmic, shrunken and cold.

It will be noticed that disturbance of the sexual function is always associated with nervous phenomena, and pathological processes in the male urethra reflexly cause very marked functional derangements.

Only the outer lips of the female genitalia are visible externally, the remaining organs which go to make up the complex sexual apparatus of woman being hidden from view, and some of them are located deep in the pelvic cavity.

This anatomical arrangement precludes a physical manifestation or alteration during congestion, or sexual excitement, and as there are no external bodily changes that are distinctive, the condition is attended only by subjective sensations, and these are not always correctly interpreted.

The complicated construction of this apparatus makes the liability to disturbance in its mechanism extremely great.

Havelock Ellis has very appropriately likened the female apparatus to that of an ordinary lock, while that of the male is represented by the key, which is not only required to fit, but must, by proper use, and after due adjustment, elicit the proper mechanism. If we imagine a time lock such as is used in modern safety deposit vaults, and which can be opened only after a given time and which requires not only a familiarity with its mechanism, but a knowledge of the proper combination, we have a fairly good analogy.

When we come to consider the internal location of this complex sexual apparatus, with its consequent more intimate relation with other vital internal organs, and when we remember that circulatory changes in the male apparatus, which is largely external, cause marked nervous and functional alterations; it becomes evident that there is far greater liability to constitutional disturbances from conditions of the sexual organs in the woman, than could reasonably be expected to occur in the man.

It is through the sympathetic, or vaso-motor nervous system, that women are affected more profoundly and far more frequently than are men, and this will explain why the great majority of modern women are, when compared with the men, the most frequent and greatest sufferers from nervous and functional disturbances.

The great intimacy between the pelvic and abdominal viscera makes disturbance of the former affect the latter, and there is nearly always intestinal derangement with congestive or inflammatory conditions of the pelvic organs.

Such affections as cervical endometritis, or inflammation of the lining of the neck of the womb, are almost invariably accompanied by digestive disturbances.

Normal digestion may be said to depend, primarily, upon innervation, or the integrity of the nerve supply. Dyspepsia, or difficult digestion, is the most common of affections and not only accompanies every acute disease, but is found in connection with a derangement of any vital organ, besides being the result of purely mental impressions. The emotions, such as fear, anger, joy, or any excitability, very frequently interfere with appetite and digestion.

The two great essentials for digestion, assimilation and nutrition, are:

First: Circulation of good blood—upon which depends secretion and absorption.

Second. Peristalsis—which is caused reflexly by a stimulus to the sympathetic nerves distributed throughout the alimentary canal.

Secretion and absorption are rendered effective by peristalsis and, indeed, the circulation is governed by the vaso-motor or sympathetic nerves.

So very intimate is the connection between the sympathetic and cerebro-spinal nervous systems, that the separation of the one from the other should be considered purely for the sake of convenience.

The various physiological processes of animal life are governed by the sympathetic system, and hence movements of the parts supplied with nerves from this system have been shown to be, in a measure at least, independent of the brain and spinal cord.

All reflex actions are essentially involuntary, though most of them admit of being modified, controlled or prevented by a voluntary effort.

Reflex actions preformed in health have a distinct purpose, and are adapted to secure some end desirable for the well-being of the body; but in disease many of them are irregular and purposeless.

This sympathetic system consists of a series of ganglia with innumerable nerve fibres.

The largest ganglia in the body, with the network or fibres, is situated in the abdomen; is known as the epigastric or solar plexus; supplies the entire abdominal viscera, and is frequently referred to as the abdominal brain.

A careful study of the anatomical arrangement of this important nervous apparatus, shows that it is connected with the thoracic portion of the system above by means of the splanchnic nerves, and also that there is a very intimate and close connection, by numerous fibres, with the plexus below which supplies the viscera of the pelvic cavity.

In the female, in whom the important organs of reproduction are located within the pelvis, there is a greater intimacy in connection than in the male, and, consequently, the digestive and generative organs are in greater sympathy, and we find a greater liability to disturbance in the digestive apparatus from alterations in the organs located in the female pelvis.

Practical exemplifications of this condition are very numerous, for not only are there reflex or sympathetic digestive disorders in pathological conditions of the sexual organs, but there are also functional disturbances in the alimentary canal which may be attributed to what should be considered physiological states of the genitals, and which occur during the female's life of menstruation.

Young women are frequently annoyed and chagrined, while exchanging caresses with a lover during courtship, by borborygmi, or more or less loud rumbling of the intestines, over which they have no control, but which causes embarrassment by its inopportune appearance at an undesirable time, and which may be ascribed to circulatory changes in the genitalia.

Intense sexual excitement or prolonged or violent intercourse in susceptible women is sometimes followed by a period of "stomach sickness."

One of the early symptoms of pregnancy, which is very common in women who are ordinarily in good health, is nausea and vomiting.

It sometimes commences almost immediately after conception and is usually present, to some extent, during the first few months of pregnancy.

It is generally most marked in women of highly nervous temperaments, and sometimes the sickness becomes so excessive as to resist all treatment and to seriously affect the patient's health, and even imperil her life.

Most authorities hold that more or less nausea is a normal and nearly constant phenomenon in pregnancy, and it is difficult to believe that nearly every woman has at all times an abnormal uterus, and so it must be considered a physiological condition rather than a disease.

This "morning sickness," which is sometimes the first intimation of the woman's condition, is without doubt not due to any lesion in the stomach or intestines, but is unquestionably the result of some change in the generative organs, slight though it may be, and is, therefore, reflex or sympathetic.

Most frequently it subsides after the fourth month, when the womb becomes markedly enlarged, and its usual onset soon after conception points to its being caused rather by vascular changes in the interior of the womb, than by any great structural enlargement of that organ.

Be that as it may, all the authorities are practically agreed that the stomach symptoms are the result of some tension, pressure or irritation of the uterine nerves.

If the slight changes in the womb during the first days of pregnancy, or those which occur with an endocervicitis, are sufficient to cause nausea and vomiting, it is not reasonable to suppose that the congestions and tension in this structure incident to sexual excitement when recurrent, prolonged and repressed (but not relieved by nature's method with orgasm) will eventually cause some nervous instability in a normal woman during her fruitful period?

Spontaneous relief from this condition is the rule

in the male, but such is not so common in the female and probably does not occur until a thorough familiarity with orgasm has been established, and then only in comparatively rare instances.

Pregnancy is also frequently accompanied by a tendency to fainting, and by mental peculiarities such as undue irritability, despondency, moroseness and various "longings" that may be unnatural.

The pelvic organs are supplied by sympathetic nerves through the hypogastric plexus, which not only receives many branches from the solar plexus, but has direct connection with the cerebro-spinal system by means of the nervi erigentes, which Gaskell terms the pelvic splanchnic nerves. A peculiarity of these nerves is that they do not first pass, like sympathetic nerves elsewhere, into ganglia, but run directly into the central nervous system, thus establishing direct communication between the hypogastric sympathetics and the brain.

The sympathetic nerves coming from the lower part of this plexus and which are distributed (according to Gray) to the rectum, bladder, seminal vesicles and the erectile tissues in the vagina, penis, etc., contain a large proportion of spinal nerve fibres.

It will thus be seen that by reason of this more direct communication between the central nervous system and the pelvic viscera, the brain has a very great influence over the pelvic organs, and, vice versa, these organs profoundly affect the mind.

Proctologists are impressed with the frequency with which comparatively small lesions in the rectum are accompanied by hypochondriasis, or undesirable mental conditions, which are altogether out of proportion to the extent of the lesion; and sexual neurasthenia in the male is of such common occurrence that we need not dwell upon it here.

Many more members of the "weaker sex" are afflicted by "nervousness" than are those of the masculine persuasion; and when we look for the causation of this well-known condition, we are prone to forget that both are subject to the same inexorable natural laws and we are too apt to be guided by misdirected sentiment, and by reason of a thoughtless want of knowledge the condition is ascribed to other and less prolific causes.

Diseased states may be considered as exaggerated or intensified physiological conditions, in which there is an added effort of nature to overcome an impediment to the performance of a natural function; or disease is the "abnormal performance of function by one or more organs or tissues."

There can be no distinct line of demarkation between health and disease, for the maintenance of a maximum or minimum physiological standard merges imperceptibly into disease and must then be considered abnormal, or pathological.

Sexual excitement, like pregnancy in women, may be considered a normal condition in mature life, and excessive frequency or absence denotes abnormality.

The natural end and aim of this excitement is copulation, which, when properly carried out, allays through orgasm the excitement to the performance of a fundamental, normal function. If there be failure of orgasm there will remain, though the excitement may subside, a want of the natural gratification which prompts the excitement; and the sympathetic nervous system, which links the physical with the mental being, will not be in a state of complete tranquility but in a condition of more or less unrest.

This obtains whether or not the individual understands or is aware of the cause, but now and again a woman may be found whose experience has taught her and who is frank enough to acknowledge that her recurrent state of nervousness is overcome by the production of an orgasm.

The number of "high strung" women, whose nervous systems are vulnerable and irritable, is apparently on the increase, and when we come to look for the causes which bring about this condition in our women, if we are inclined to be thorough and scientific, we should not ignore the great influence of the sexual function, nor fail to consider their sexual relations and habits.

CHAPTER VII.

SEXUAL HABITS IN THE MARRIED

Conversation and Sexual Habits—Percentage of Childless Marriages—The Course of Nature Would Increase Family about every Two Years—Celibacy with Marriage—Love for Children Grows with Presence—Time of Greatest Desire the Auspicious Time for Conception—Family Growth Governs Sexual Acts—Women who Must not only Subdue their own Feelings, but Resist Husband for One-half of Month—Withdrawal Common but not Satisfactory—Effects of Woman's Sacrifice—The Condom—The use of Douches—Employment of Suppositories, Injections, Sponges, Pessaries, etc.—Untoward Effects of their Use—Fear as a Cause of Suppression—Monthly Regulators—Active Measures for Interrupting Pregnancy have for Object Emptying of Womb—Methods of the Abortionist—Immediate Dangers and After Effects.

Ordinary statements about sexual habits are not at all reliable, and conversation has been trained with so much care that it can be guaranteed, except in rare instances, not to betray the innermost thoughts and private acts.

An unbiased analysis of conduct in society reveals the startling fact, and warrants the assertion that life, as it is usually seen, is, in the aggregate, very largely composed of actions that are the result of hypocrisy and hysterics, and this becomes emphasized when we consider the feminine sexual life.

Conditions prevail and are so plainly evident that the guardians of the nation are forced to confront them, and the question of "race suicide" has agitated the minds of the thoughtful. Speaking to a committee of the inter-church conference on marriage and divorce, the President is reported to have recently said:

"Questions like the tariff and the currency are of literally no consequence whatsoever compared with the vital question of having the unit of our social life, the home, preserved. It is impossible to overstate the importance of the cause you represent.

"If the average husband and wife rulfill their duties toward one another and toward their children as Christianity teaches them, then we may rest absolutely assured that the other problems will solve themselves. But if we have solved every other problem in the wisest possible way, it shall profit us nothing if we have lost our own national soul; and we will have lost it if we do not have the question of the relations of the family put upon the proper basis.

"I can say in advance that so far as within me lies all will be done to co-operate with you toward the end that you have in view. One of the most unpleasant and dangerous features of our American life is the diminishing bith rate and the loosening of the marital ties among the old native American families.

"It goes without saying that for the race as for the

individual no material prosperity, no business growth, no artistic or scientific development, will count, if the race commits suicide. Therefore, I count myself fortunate in having the chance to work with you in this matter of vital importance to the national welfare."

When shorn of sentiment, the most prolific cause of this state of affairs will be found in willful family limitations, and inasmuch as women are the bearers of children, the question devolves upon their sexual habits.

Hand in hand with the decreasing number of children, is found an increasing number of neurasthenics, and it is a false gallantry and mistaken modesty that attributes this condition to less prolific and more remote causes.

There can be only two sensible reasons for sterilty or restricted families:

First. Physical inability, which nearly always means disease.

Second. Want of natural copulation, or inhibition of growth.

Generally speaking, the constitutional conditions that cause sterility, with the possible exception of syphilis, are so few that in nearly all instances this defect may be attributed to previous or existing derangement of the genitalia.

A certain small per cent. of the cases in which the women are sterile may be due to congenital or acquired malformations, but the vast majority may be ascribed to inflammatory conditions.

Practically, the greater number of cases are due primarily to some kind of infection, and the prevalence of diseases of women, innocently acquired, as they very often are, is not altogether flattering to the morals of our society.

In giving the causes of inflammatory conditions of the female pelvic organs, Pozzi has this to say in regard to copulation:

"Excessive coitus, whether during menstruation or coincident with great fatigue, may provoke uterine inflammation independently of all contamination; but far more often it is a gonorrhœal infection, more or less disregarded, which is so efficient a cause of metritis and which plays this role in the case of newly married women. Husbands who consider themselves cured and pay no attention to a trifling urethral discharge, may thus infect the urethra, the vagina, the cervical and uterine cavities, and the tubes of the young wife. Such a gonorrhœal infection may remain a long time latent within the cervix; then under the irritation of a rough examination, or after abortion or labor, the infection gains entrance to the body of the uterus. Nœggerath asserts that in women with gonorrhœa, abortion and labor are followed by metritis and perimetritis as often as 75 per cent.; substituting salpingitis for perimetritis, the statement is not exaggerated. It is doubtless to this cause, also, rather than to the traumatism of too frequent coitus, that we must refer the metritis of prostitutes. Abortions are frequent and unheeded among women who are beginning a debauched life, and later the inflammation of the uterus rises high enough to involve the tubes, obliterating them and causing sterility."

It has been customary to lay the blame for the

woman's short-coming upon the husband in a great many instances, for it is held that though he may be competent to perform his marital duties, yet the seminal fluid may be deficient in the required spermatozoa.

It must be acknowledged that a large proportion of men have at some time in their career been afflicted with veneral disease, but that they are thereby permanently disabled is very far from being the rule and must be considered a rare exception.

It is conceivable that epididymitis, which sometimes follows gonorrhœal infection, might render the man sterile, but it would necessarily have to be double, and, in any event, so severe as to destroy the integrity of the tubules.

The conclusions of different authorities in regard to the relative frequency of sterility are so widely different that any positive statements would not be warranted.

For the purpose of this discussion it is sufficient to state that the number of marriages that have at all times been involuntarily fruitless is comparatively small, and would probably not exceed two or three per cent. of the whole.

Given two people in ordinary health and living together under natural and proper conditions, it is reasonably safe to assume that if nature were permitted to take its unrestricted course there would, with some exceptions, ordinarily be an addition to the family once every two or three years during the childbearing period.

Evidences of "restriction" are on every hand, for

the periodical advent of the addition has ceased to be the rule among the educated, and that this condition is not wholly unpremeditated goes without saying.

Human nature is the same to-day as it always has been, and hopes of its greatly changing cannot be entertained, and so a little reflection will convince the observer that limited families are desirable by parents.

Without considering the moral aspect, we are brought to the conclusion that, in order to attain the end desired, either the most natural copulation is avoided (with a view to the prevention of conception) or pregnancy is interrupted.

Viewing the effect upon health and well-being only, and with no desire to fix the responsibility, it is evident that the woman is the one more largely concerned and is by far the greatest sufferer under these conditions.

A life of celibacy cannot be said to be a natural one, and when this state of celibacy is combined with propinquity, in which there must of necessity be a source of repeated and more or less constant sexual excitability, there is added to the already incomplete life a greater burden of increased tension, which must be a very considerable factor in the causation of unrest, or nervousness.

If one is removed from the possibility of external influences to sexual excitement and has only to subdue the spontaneous promptings, there is comparatively little to overcome and practically no temptation to resist, and hence there will be little or no discomfort felt; but if one is repeatedly and more or less continuously subjected to excitement and thrown amidst the natural facilities for its abatement, but is called upon to forego the opportunity to satisfy an urgent demand, the situation becomes entirely changed.

There is no energy required in the restraint of that upon which no force is exerted.

The vitality expended during nervous tranquility is nothing when compared to the exhaustion of nervous tension.

The woman who has not been thrilled by the caress of a lover, and has not experienced the profound effects of physiological copulation, knows nothing of the almost superhuman efforts required to forever resist when occasions and opportunities are pressing.

Just as there is a vast difference between the virtue of ignorance and freedom from temptation, and the virtue of information and opportunity; so also are the effects of ungratified desires, which are the frequent results of surroundings, far greater than the nervous disturbances occasioned by the intrinsic promptings of single life.

Perhaps the greatest concern of the majority of women who are having sexual relations is whether or not they have become "caught," which they usually determine by the appearance of their menstruation.

Pregnancy marks a very important epoch in a woman's career, and it is but natural that it should cause her great anxiety.

It is ridiculous to assume that any mature woman could be ignorant of the manner in which maternity is reached, and if the incentive to copulation is recognized (and the existing feelings, which are but temporary, cannot be ignored) thoughts of what may follow upon the natural completion of the act will be forthcoming.

However great the desire for offspring may be, there will be conditions to influence a preference for timely occurrence, and this would be regulated if the situation could be controlled.

When people do not have sexual intercourse it may be ascribed to one of the following reasons:

First. They live under conditions that prevent it.

Second. They have not the physical qualifications.

Third. They are not of the proper age.

Fourth. They live amidst surroundings that are unfavorable.

Fifth. They are not normal human beings.

How many of our people there are nowadays who live throughout the course of their married lives without any attempt to interfere with the course of nature in their sexual relations, we will not presume to say, but the conviction is forced upon us that the proportion is very small among the knowing ones.

Some attempts looking to family limitations, however ridiculous and ineffective they may be, are, as a rule, at one time or another, made by women of intelligence who are exposed to conception.

All children born are by no means the result of deliberate intentions.

The number of accidental conceptions is certainly very large, for, excepting those who believe themselves free from susceptibility, the momentous question with the young matron for the time being is, "whether or not she will come around."

This solicitude it natural and not without some justification, for there are many conditions in which rapid childbearing would prove detrimental, albeit the tendency at present is in the other direction.

Were it not for the wise provision that makes the love for offspring grow with their presence, there would be many more undesirable children, and cases of neglect would be greatly multiplied.

How best to circumvent family complications is the burning question of the hour with the average young wife, and a satisfactory solution of this problem would be a boon to society and prevent untold suffering.

When confronted with the question, the usual answer is, in effect, "be natural," which in these days of stress is no answer at all, as it is not practical.

The duties to self, husband, family, society, church and state are very numerous, conflicting and exacting; and so they are usually considered, if at all, in approximately the order named.

Married women of mature age and living the ordinary life may for convenience be divided into three classes:

First. Those who follow their natural inclinations in their sexual relations without regard to what may follow.

Second. Those who resort to some means for the prevention of conception.

Third. Those in whom pregnancy is interrupted.

It is idle to promulgate lofty theories and sentiments when we are brought face to face with conditions that must be practically dealt with.

Either the American people are becoming markedly less prolific, or else their sexual habits have greatly changed during the past few decades, for the average size of families has greatly decreased since previous generations.

When it is recalled that the time of greatest sexual desire is also the time when conception is most apt to take place, it will be found that, generally speaking, the women in the first class are today in the minority.

Nearly, if not quite all, intelligent and normal women will, at some time in their career, feel some hesitancy about having natural and complete sexual intercourse.

Many, more or less habitually, refrain entirely from relations during that time of the month in which they believe themselves exposed.

Others are careful and intend to prevent undesirable results by not completing the act in the natural way.

Not a few take some measure which they hope to be effective in preventing conception, and a considerble proportion resort to some means for interrupting pregnancy after it has begun.

Most frequently the husband is consulted with a view to co-operation, and a reliance upon his care and assistance in carrying out the design to defeat propagation, so far as their conscience permits and their knowledge and ability goes, is secured.

Of course, there is always a certain number of the

so-called "uneducated" and unthinking ones who give little or no thought to their future, but as civilization advances this number decreases, and to-day it is comparatively small.

Very many have conscientious scruples against active measures, or are fearful of, and deterred by, disastrous results which they have known to come from "meddling"; and the inability to secure reliable aid, together with the personal and social effects of questionable practices, influences and conduct when relief from responsibility is considered.

The anxieties and sacrifices which this phase of the sexual habits entails is tremendous and cannot be ignored.

Other things being equal, the greatest degree of domestic felicity would be found where both of the parties directly interested were given the greatest sexual freedom, and at the same time have a family of desirable size.

It is beyond our purpose to consider anything but the mental and physical well-being of the two people directly interested.

Regardless of whether or not it be an established fact, the impression seems to prevail quite extensively that a woman will conceive only if she have intercourse during a certain time in the month—which is determined by her menstruation—but for the remainder of the time she is free from this liability—and many act on that belief.

The time limit is somewhat varied, but is held to be approximately one-half of the month.

That period beginning from six to ten days after

menstruation has ceased, and extending to from one to three days before the onset of the next menstrual flow, is pretty generally considered to be the time when there is little or no liability to conception.

This rule does not apply to all women and is not absolutely true, but nevertheless it determines, to a great extent, the sexual relations, and the acts of very many are governed accordingly.

When a woman is menstruating she is considered "unwell" and the mental impression of uncleanness suggested by the discharge, for which there is a natural aversion, tends to inhibit free sexual congress at this time.

It is not so much the want of desire on the part of the woman as it is the consciousness of being unfit, or the fear of contaminating or causing disgust, that prevents the proper mood for intercourse.

Not seldom passionate women will tolerate or invite relations when there is some show of menstrual discharge and afterwards plead ignorance of their condition and excuse their conduct with profuse apologies when evidence of the bloody discharge becomes exposed. Not infrequently there will be some "staining" when the woman believes herself to be free, for the added congestion incident to excitement and coitus enhances the flow and occasions concern, not only by reason of the natural aversion to the discharge, but by a popular belief among the laity that it is contaminating and may by contact cause disease.

Probably for these reasons principally, intercourse

during the time when there are signs of menstruation is not so very common.

Personal discomforts, social life and financial conditions engender a dread of pregnancy, and in some cases this becomes so formidable as to counteract the pleasures to be derived from intercourse, and not only prevents a mood for its enjoyment, but actually keeps some couples from yielding to their promptings at the time when they believe the woman to be exposed to this condition.

This is usually the time when the physical condition is such that the spontaneous desires are urgent, and in fact many women, when left to themselves and not subjected to external influences, feel sexually inclined at this time only, for at other times their desires must be actively aroused, which, if done at all, is accomplished with more or less difficulty.

An attractive and healthy woman must not only subdue and overcome her own feelings during this period, which in itself involves the exercise of considerable will-power and self-denial, but she must in addition successfully withstand and resist the importunities of the husband whose presence is mutually exciting, and who is to her, in this respect, the man above all men.

These recurrent anatomical conditions, which are natural and physiological, create a state of undue tension extending not unusually over nearly half of the month, and a considerable amount of vitality is expended without any benefit, but with the loss of, not only a great deal of nervous energy, but also the ability to successfully copulate when the time which is considered safe arrives. The constant dripping of emotion that requires resistance, sooner or later wears away the stone of stability and leaves a weakened nervous system to govern the normal functions—which means a want of harmony in action.

The widely prevalent practice of yielding to desire and inviting a state of sexual excitement, though not completing the act in a natural way, but suddenly terminating it by withdrawal before the critical moment arrives, is undertaken with a willful determination to prevent the possibility of resulting pregnancy.

The sensations of excitement are so alluring that it is difficult to forego the incidental pleasure, and it is by a prearranged plan that the actions are undertaken and governed.

A reliance must be had upon the man, for on him depends the carrying out of the plan.

As the results of this practice are somewhat different in the female than in the male, some women may, after a time, come to be a party to the procedure more from a desire to please than from personal gratification derived, for they tend to become not only indifferent but are actually disgusted and have it over with as quickly as they can, with the feeling of performing a disagreeable duty.

The effect upon the man who assumes the responsibility to thus "care" for the woman, is very largely the same as that which results from any other method of artificial orgasm.

Manhood rebels against an unnatural interference with a sacred right, and the repeated outrage of manhood cannot be salutary but must be detrimental.

In view of the fact that any seminal emission that is not within the vaginal passage becomes disgusting to a normal man, however effectively it may allay excitement, this practice can in no sense be ennobling, but must detract from masculinity.

The inevitable consciousness of lustful selfish indulgence predisposes to a disturbed mind and, instead of developing harmony, causes discord.

The climax of the sexual act is in itself involuntary, but by training and an effort of the will, the orgasm may be hastened or retarded.

Since personal pleasure alone is sought, the orgasm is postponed as long as possible, but the intensity of the emotion prevents the limit being accurately measured, and so it sometimes happens that a portion of the emission inadvertently finds its way into the vagina.

This difficulty to control the existing condition partially accounts for the frequency of accidental conceptions.

The constitutional effects of this practice in the man are usually not greatly unlike those of natural copulation, but the restriction, together with the comparative passivity of the woman, greatly detracts from the gratification.

At all events, the beneficial effects cannot be compared to those of normal coitus.

Orgasm in woman is usually of slower development than in man, and, like all involuntary acts, is capable of being more or less modified by the will.

When coitus interruptus is intended there will naturally be a lack of eagerness on the part of the wife and, in consequence, this stage is usually not reached at all by her.

Were the woman to display a natural ardor and act in accordance with its inclination, it would be difficult for the man to effect a timely withdrawal, and so she assumes a careless and passive attitude which results in a failure to reach the climax.

She takes some part, passive though it may be, in whatever preliminaries there are, and consciously submits to the maneuvers undertaken with perhaps an antagonistic mental struggle, but with a resultant circulatory change in the genitalia.

She is agitated by emotions which are a possible mingling of fear and desire, and her perturbation, instead of being relieved by an explosive orgasm, is intensified and turned into disgust by the revolting sensation of an excretion deposited upon her exterior. Instead of relaxation, with a body tingling under an invigorated and equalized circulation, her rest is disturbed by undue tension, her mind filled with reproaches and her senses disgusted, while outraged but kindly nature struggles to restore tranquility.

What she deems a sacrifice has failed to satisfy her consort, brought upon herself a loathing for the things that she should cherish, and until her sex again asserts itself she feels dissatisfied with life, considers herself a martyr and marriage a failure.

If she be fortunate enough to have previously experienced the profound effects and sensations of physiological copulation, her recurrent cycle of physical fitness awakens memories that overshadow and blot out her disappointment; but if she has no knowledge of these and there be frequent repetition of acts that give no pleasure and satisfaction, she gradually drifts into a life of increasing miseries.

The unpleasant effects and the uncertainty of a timely interruption of coitus have led to the use of other and various measures for the prevention of conception, the most common of which are:

1. The use of condoms.
2. The employment of douches.
3. The insertion of suppositories.
4. The injection of antiseptics.
5. The wearing of sponges or pessaries.

The condom, or sheath of thin rubber, is in extensive use and commonly sold "for the prevention of disease only."

It is a sack of thin rubber which is drawn over the male organ preparatory to copulation, and besides detracting greatly from the pleasure and satisfaction derived, is not always at hand, and when so, not easily and agreeably adjusted, and is liable to burst under the force exerted, which of course, destroys its efficacy.

Douches are in very common use.

Water of different temperatures, and sometimes with the addition of an antiseptic or acid, such as vinegar, is used with the hope of washing out or sterilizing the seminal fluid.

The walls of the vagina are normally in contact with each other and their mucous lining is thrown into numerous folds, thus making a thorough irrigation somewhat difficult.

The activity of the womb during the orgasm permits of an immediate entrance of a portion of the vital fluid into the organ, which cannot then be reached with the ordinary methods employed.

These, together with the natural tendency to rest after the act is completed, and the indisposition of the woman to bother with the inconvenience of its use, help to render the procedure problematical.

The temperature of the water, the strength of the solution, the implements used and the carelessness of administration not infrequently cause local injury.

Various suppositories and injections into the vagina, containing what is meant to sterilize the semen, are introduced into the vaginal passage prior to the act.

It should be remembered that whatever is sufficient to destroy germs is also strong enough to act injuriously upon the tissues in which the germs thrive.

Soft rubber "womb supporters," or "night caps," which are intended to fit over the neck of the womb; stem pessaries of rubber or aluminum, to be inserted into the canal of the cervix, and sponges with a string attached to facilitate removal, are often used to prevent entrance of spermatozoa into the uterus, and left for a varying period.

The ordinary woman is not able to insert one of these instruments with any degree of accuracy even if she has been instructed how to proceed, for it requires not only a knowledge of the parts but some skill to properly adjust a pessary, and this is not possessed by either herself or husband.

The upper part of the vagina is spacious and a

sponge of ordinary size could easily be pushed beyond the mouth of the womb by the male organ, and probably this is what usually happens.

Even if those articles which are designed to serve as an impediment to the passage of the semen into the womb are properly used during intercourse, there still remains the possibility of pregnancy after their removal, if spermatozoa are present in the vagina.

Stem pessaries are liable to cause inflammation, and any foreign body in the vagina tends to injure the male as well as the female by the friction incident to the movements; but notwithstanding the inconvenience of their use and their failure to positively insure security, they nevertheless largely counteract the fear so generally entertained, and are more or less widely used.

Doubtless one or another of the foregoing methods are at some time or other employed by many women who are fearful of exposure, and we cannot shut our eyes to the fact that they are more or less successful in accomplishing their purpose.

One has but to note the numerous advertisements of medicines for the relief of suppressed menstruation to be convinced that their use at the present time is very large.

There is no known medicine which, when taken into the system in non-poisonous doses, has a sufficient specific action on the womb to cause this organ to empty its contents when pragnancy has begun in a healthy woman who has not previously miscarried.

These so-called monthly regulators contain drugs that have a purgative effect and act more or less violently on the pelvic viscera, and as the womb is placed close beside the rectum it is liable to some disturbance when this viscus is greatly irritated.

That miscarriage is sometimes produced by enormous doses of such drugs cannot be denied, but their action is not upon the womb alone, but is the result of constitutional disturbance, and their use is further dangerous in that they establish a predisposition to miscarry that makes it very difficult for a woman to subsequently bear a child if she so desires and has once miscarried.

Very often these regulators are apparently effective when pregnancy does not really exist, and the suppression is caused by the fear of the woman who has been exposed and whose mental condition of concentration is itself sufficient to delay the flow.

Pozzi, a well known French authority on diseases of women, says upon the subject of amenorrhœa, or suppressed menstruation.

"The condition of the nervous system has a decided influence upon the production amenorrhœa. Fright may cause a temporary suspension of the menses. On the other hand, there are cases on record in which amenorrhœa has been cured by some sudden emotion. The amenorrhœa of prisoners and of insane women confined to asylums is due as much to the mental depression as to the anæmia consequent upon seclusion. Chlorosis, which causes amenorrhœa, seems to be a disease of the nervous system. Absence of menstruation is often noted in the hysterical. Sudden chilling, which is often given as a cause of amenorrhœa, probably acts through the vaso-motor tract.

The emotional amenorrhœa of the newly married, or of women who are very desirous of having children, is probably to be referred to the inhibitory power of the nervous system; its occurrence simultaneously with tympanites has often been the cause of bitter disappointment. Anxiety may induce amenorrhœa in women who, because of the irregularities of their lives or from some other reason, dread pregnancy. I have seen several instances of this. The last two forms may be due in part to auto-suggestion."

When women are determined to avoid the responsibilities of motherhood they occasionally resort to self-inflicted physical violence to further their aim.

A severe tax upon the system by disease, overexertion or shock sometimes brings on uterine activity and causes the womb to empty itself, but this strain must, in ordinary cases, necessarily be of sufficient severity to endanger life.

The habit of using hot injections, hot sitz baths, etc., is usually only effective in that by doing so the patient relieves her mind by the work and discomfort caused, but it is hardly probable that she would in this manner inflict sufficient injury upon herself to interrupt pregnancy if it actually existed.

That an increasing number of women resort to active local measures to relieve themselves of a supposed burden cannot be gainsaid, and that a certain per cent., surprisingly small though it may appear when the dangers are considered, subsequently suffer very much by so doing and sometimes pay the extreme penalty, is strikingly evident.

Whatever the local method made use of to inhibit

fœtal growth may be, it has for its object the emptying of the uterine cavity.

This is usually brought about by in some manner mechanically interfering with the womb and exciting it to sufficient activity to expel its contents.

When the uterus is in itself not able to discharge all of the fruits of conception and some remnants of the growth remain within its cavity, disastrous results are very likely to follow, if the remains be not removed.

The retention of some of the products of conception occurs frequently and the putrefactive changes place the woman in a most dangerous condition. In this event, the only hope of saving the woman's life lies in an immediate operative procedure, which not seldom proves to be of no avail.

That serious results do not more frequently follow miscarriages is probably due to the fact that the great majority occur in the early months, and up to the end of the third month the ovum is generally cast off in one mass, the decidua subsequently coming away in shreds, or as an entire membrane.

Playfair says: "At a very early period of pregnancy the ovum is cast off with such facility, and is of such minute size, that the fact of an abortion having occurred passes unrecognized. Very many cases in which the patient goes one or two weeks over her time, and then has what is supposed to be merely a more than usually profuse period, are probably instances of such miscarriages. Velpeau detected an ovum of about fourteen days which was not larger than an ordinary pea, and it is easy to understand how so small a body should pass unnoticed in the blood which escapes along with it."

The two great immediate dangers of miscarriage are hemmorrhage, and inflammation due to the absorption of septic material.

When the abortion is voluntary there is the added risk of introducing the poison that may cause a septic condition.

A great loss of blood may seriously affect the patient, and inflammation, if at all severe, is likely to cause more or less permanent injury and, when extensive, produce a fatality.

Miscarriage is considered so lightly and the longing for relief is so great, that some women will, in desperation, when they are unable to obtain assistance, attempt to produce this condition by themselves.

This is an extremely dangerous practice and any woman who is rash enough to resort to it may consider herself extremely fortunate if she escapes the most serious consequences.

When intelligently carried out, as sometimes becomes necessary, the procedure is undertaken with surgical asepsis and the neck of the womb is usually sufficiently stretched to permit of ready passage, when some instrument such as a sound, bougie, catheter, plug or strip of gauze is introduced into the uterus to disturb its tranquility and bring on contractions.

More or less pain and hemmorrhage is caused, and after a time there will be expulsion of the uterine contents, and if this be complete and no complications arise the purpose will have been accomplished.

In nearly every community one or more persons may be found who can be induced to assist in this nefarious practice and their number indicates the frequency with which such services are demanded, while their prosperity bespeaks the lucrativeness of the business.

The enforcement of enacted laws which would incriminate all classes of society in considerable numbers is impractical, and so this, like its twin vice, prostitution, becomes a necessary evil which can only be eradicated by the reconstruction of humanity, and only diminished by the education of the people along other than the customary lines.

That the sexual habits of the married are far from being ideal, but that neither sex is blameless, and that a great deal of additional happiness would be found if a little more knowledge were had and frankness observed, is illustrated by the following extract from the Woman's Magazine:

"What a good thing it would be if women would be true to themselves and converse intelligently when in the society of gentlemen. There is nothing that honest men desire more than to understand that mysterious race that is so like themselves and yet so unlike, who share their homes, but not their thoughts; who are so shrewd, so practical and so irrational. The poor men yearn to break down the invisible barrier and see into the real life of these they love so well; but the loved ones smile and chatter and say pretty things, and ingenious things, they have borrowed from men and improved in the borrowing, but never a word of the really true and in many instances vital thoughts that are working in their busy brains. So the men flatter and lie because they think the women like it, and the women accept it all because they think it is man's nature; and the men think the women are dear empty-headed angels; and women think men are fine, intelligent brutes; and the two classes go on loving and despising one another accordingly, and all for the want of a little discernment and truthfulness in conversation."

CHAPTER VIII

HYGIENIC SEXUAL RELATIONS

Family Welfare Depends Upon Sexual Relations—Ability and Timely Exercise Necessary—Play of the Imagination—Personal Care—Timely Avoidance of Intimate Relations—Importance of Sense of Touch—Hesitancy upon Contact Before Vigorous Activity—Size of Organs has Greatest Effect on Mind—Essentials of Female Conduct and Male Actions—Impulse Expressed by Female Clinging and by Encircling Traction of Male—Sense of Touch Requires Bodily Wave—Simultaneous Climax Reached by Intelligent Co-operation—Conditions that Influence Desire—Delay of Orgasm and Woman's Pleasure—Causes of Excess—Previous Habits a Guide to Frequency—Capacity and Proficiency Acquired by Practice—Nature's Supply of Seed Unlimited and only a Portion Elaborated—First Attempts not Successful—Failure Attributed to Active Party and Mental Effect Bad—Entrance does not mean Copulation—Success depends upon Husband's Conduct—Women of the "Half World" and their Habits Compared with Others—Frequent Excitations Primarily Injurious—Sexual Capacity as Various as the Digestive—Normal Frequency of Relations—Sexual Excesses Highly Improbable in Women without Undue Stimulation—Influence of Prolonged Continence.

What the proper sexual relations are, and how to establish and maintain them, vitally concerns adult humanity and especially those persons who are passing through the first years of their married lives.

Marriage implies a desire for the exercise of the sexual function, with its concomitant pleasures and results, and if these be but partially, or not at all realized, its primary object is defeated and it must be a failure.

Upon the proper exercise of this function depends, more than all else, the mental and physical well-being of the principals, and consequently the family welfare, which is of the greatest importance to all, is directly concerned.

It is not to be presumed that two people would, under ordinary circumstances, voluntarily assume the marital relation if they could not tolerate each other's presence and, instead of growing apart, they would, if their sexual relations were satisfactory, naturally become more needful and necessarily more deeply attached to one another as their relations continued and their lives progressed.

Two things are necessary for physiological copulation—the ability to do so, and also the proper and timely exercise of this ability.

In a game of baseball it is not enough for a player to be able to make a run, but it is also necessary for him to exercise this ability and run at the opportune time if he expects to make a score, and so if the copulators intend to make the act count the team must work together and be active in the nick of time.

When the male is unable to perform the sexual act he is termed impotent, and when the female cannot bear children the condition is called sterility.

A man may be sterile and yet be able to perform the act, but if he be impotent he is necessarily sterile by reason of his impotency, and so it is usual to understand the term impotency, as applying to the male only, but if we use the word in reference to having physiological copulation, then many women are also impotent, and that without any regard to their sterility.

A woman may fulfill her physiological function without any subjective sexual satisfaction, for neither sexual desire nor orgasm are necessary to fecundity, and that very many women of the better class do live thus passively is only too true, however sad it may be.

Sexual desire and orgasm must have been experienced by both parties if copulation is to be considered successful and complete.

Sexuality should be regarded as a dual entity involving both the mind and the body, one part being concerned in originating the impulse and the other in the gratification of the desire.

The first is a general function, closely allied to nutrition and largely dependent upon surroundings and impressions; while the second is the outward evidence or local manifestation of its existence.

The general consciousness of sex is a natural endowment, and arises from a special function impressed upon every cell in the normal individual.

By the exercise of the imagination, which this consciousness of sex affords, ideals and images are spontaneously formed and these become mirrored and more or less accurately reflected by some member of the opposite sex, and thus desire which becomes individualized, results from a play of imagination and association of ideas.

It is obvious that anticipations of responsiveness

are delightful and desirous, and that personal desire and gratification become largely imaginary; so in order to enhance and preserve desirable conditions it is of advantage to permit of a drawing upon the imagination.

Any act or condition of the object of desire that is offensive to the senses has a tendency to give a shock to the imagination and prevent its play in the formation of exalted sexual feeling and should, therefore, be studiously avoided.

Suggestive or coquettish conduct is alluring only so far as not to encroach upon vulgarity, and though the imagination should be fed and given sufficient range, yet if it be not guarded by partial concealment of charms and motives until the opportune time, there is danger of destroying the sexual lure by interrupting the anticipations with premature revelations.

Feminine charms become such, to a certain extent, by the manner in which they are used, for an untimely and sudden display of physical attractions is fatal to the imagination, and not seldom occasions revulsion.

One of the most important things to consider and observe in the maintenance of desirable sexual relations is scrupulous personal cleanliness.

The excretions of the body are offensive and emit disgusting odors.

This is particularly true of the secretions of the genital organs, which rapidly accumulate and become obnoxious and their presence, which is usually only noticed at times when congress is intended, almost invariably creates unfavorable impressions which are associated with the individual, as well as with the act itself. To prevent disgust for both, cleanly habits must at all times be observed.

When for any reason free and natural intercourse is intended to be limited, it is preferable and advisable to have the parties occupy separate beds during the times of such restriction.

This separation will prevent undue excitability which is aroused by close bodily contact in suggestive attire and amidst most favorable surroundings for the performance of the sexual act.

Circumstances make little acts of endearment mean different things and cause them to have varied effects.

The chaste kiss imprinted at the time of parting conveys a vastly different significance and has an effect nothing like that of the warm, clinging embrace after retiring, which naturally leads to progressive acts with their increasing emotion and physical excitation.

We never value our freedom so highly as when we are threatened with or made to feel its curtailment, and when one is passionate but forced to restrain oneself there is disappointment and a tendency to resentment which lingers more or less indefinitely.

It is expecting too much to look for the exercise of reason and discretion when there is a state of excitement, and wisdom dictates the avoidance of conditions which will ensue upon intimate relations that will be without compensation.

The state of the bladder influences the erectility of the verile organ.

When this viscus is filled with the urinary excretion, which occurs in the early morning hours, there is commonly a more or less vigorous state of erection in this organ, which is realized upon awakening, and which directs the thoughts toward the marriage relation.

Men as well as women are prone to look after what they consider their marital rights or privileges, any infringements of which are not helpful to harmony; and too many husbands when in a state of physical ability help themselves to the convenient wife, and more or less selfishly use a sacred privilege to the family's detriment, but would, were the conditions such as to render the opportunity less ready, forget their "rights" or at least less frequently abuse them if they were farther removed.

Not only is unsatisfied desire provocative of immediate anger in some instances, but it also tends to make the occupants of the marriage bed less eager for subsequent efforts and makes them less proficient; and, inasmuch as one complete, physiological intercourse with its profound reaction is more productive of good than a score of partial successes, it is better to avoid constant and undue familiarity by timely separation, and limit the times of intimate contact to those periods when freedom is mutual and unrestrained.

The sense of touch is the means by which copulation is made effective.

This sense renders us conscious of the presence of a stimulus, from the slightest to the most intense degree of its action, by that indescribable something which we call feeling, or sensation.

The modifications of this sense depend largely on

the condition and extent of the parts that are affected.

In those parts of the body which have delicate tactile sensibility the epidermis which covers the nerve endings is very thin, but where the thickness of the skin is increased, as by a callus, the sense of touch is very much dulled.

The acuteness of this sense also depends upon the cutaneous circulation.

When the surface of the skin is covered by a layer of foreign material, even though it be very thin, sensibility is greatly diminished, as is readily shown by the intervention of clothing.

During sexual excitement there is not only an increased blood supply in the sexual centers, which adds to their sensibility, but the entire cutaneous circulation is increased and the skin rendered more sensitive.

The effects of coitus are not only local but constitutional also, and in order to have copulation most effective and obtain the greatest intensity of feeling, there should be nothing to interfere with the tactile sensibility; and, therefore, the most profound effects are attainable only when there is no interference by wearing apparel, and nothing but the bed clothes should be made use of if copulation is to be most complete.

A prudish disregard of this readily demonstrable fact is responsible for the loss of a great deal of that which is so effectively binding.

An increased circulation produces a greater degree of acuteness in sensibility.

Though a light touch and gentleness are at first

required, and harshness or force is painful and fatal to enjoyment; deep pressure, vigorous action and even rough treatment are desirable and often craved as the climax is being approached.

In the beginning of the local hyperæmia in the female there is a corresponding increase of sensitiveness, but the secretion, which serves as lubrication to the parts, becomes more profuse as the condition is prolonged and intensified.

If care and gentleness be not exercised when the rigid and unyielding male member is first brought in contact with the delicate and hypersensitive tissues that have not yet become adequately lubricated, the sudden and forceful stretching of the parts causes acute pain, which interrupts progression and prevents pleasurable co-operation.

This peculiarity makes hasty action appear brutal, and very much suffering is entailed by ignorance of this condition or want of consideration, especially in the first attempts.

Besides the immediate shock and pain, unfavorable impressions are retained and too often prolonged indefinitely, and fear and dread of repetition take the place of what would otherwise be joyful anticipation.

In order to elicit the keenest expectancy, slight hesitancy should be observed upon contact and gentle skirmishing undertaken before entrance is effected, after which deep pressure and more vigorous activity will be indicated.

Some apprehension is occasionally expressed about the size of the genitalia, and in general it may be said of the male organ that it rarely, if indeed ever, occurs that the member is of such monstrous size that it cannot be accommodated.

The female organs are of such elastic construction that great distension is permissible, with more or less free movability of the internal organs when these are not diseased.

When it is recalled that a child, which is certainly many times larger than a penis, is passed out of the parts, no fear need be entertained about capaciousness if ordinary care be exercised.

As a matter of fact, the chief effect of the dimensions of the parts is the impression which they make upon the mind of the observer.

The distribution of the sensory nerves is such that feeling is confined principally to the external organs of generation and the lower part of the vagina, for the upper and larger portion of this organ, together with the womb, etc., are comparatively insensible in their normal condition.

The surgeon frequently seizes the womb with a sharp instrument and pulls it down in order to enable him to get a better view of this structure, without the woman being aware of what is taking place, though the womb is made to bleed and often lacerated by the instrument in doing so.

When a woman has once born a child the cervix never again assumes exactly its previous condition, while the fourchette is almost invariably ruptured and the orifice of the vagina, and sometimes the perineum are more or less altered; but this does not necessarily impair the copulative capacity nor detract from its effectiveness if the proper attitude is taken.

The seat of pleasurable sensation, or the most sensitive areas, are the clitoris and the lower part of the vagina, but more especially the anterior wall in the neighborhood of the orifice.

Pressure or friction upon these parts determines very largely the intensity of sensation.

In the natural state and when not distended, the anterior and posterior vaginal walls are in close contact, and in any event, regardless of the size of the vaginal orifice, the woman is enabled, by the apposition of her lower limbs, to exert any desirable pressure or gripping upon the penetrating copulative member, and produce contact with and friction upon those points which have the greatest number of sensory nerve endings, and thereby increase the intensity of feeling to the climax.

As previously stated, the over or under size of the organs makes in practice but little difference except insofar as it impresses the mind, for the degree of success attained depends, more than all else, upon the efficient use of the several possessions.

In the case of the woman, the parts directly concerned in the action permit of great distension and may, with proper knowledge, be made to adjust themselves to any desirable degree of closeness; while in the case of the male any size that will permit of successful vaginal intromission is, with sufficient rigidity and dexterous manipulation, fully adequate to elicit the responses sought and be altogether effective.

The position assumed during the performance of the act may in some instances govern, to a certain extent, its success.

The size, weight and rotundity of figure will sometimes influence the convenience and closeness of the required bodily contact.

Whatever position in a given case permits of pressure and friction upon the points of greatest sensitiveness with the least exertion and discomfort, is the one that should be chosen.

Habit and the idea of closest juxtaposition lead to the assumption of different postures in different cases.

Ordinarily the feminine dorsal position is the one of natural selection and is probably the one most frequently taken.

The feminine impulse is such that at the height of desire there is an inclination for invagination, which is made possible only by a separation of the extremities and sometimes facilitated by more or less tilting of the pelvis; and then ensues a desire for the furtherance and maintenance of the ensheathed organ, which finds an expression by "clinging."

The masculine impulse prompts at first to entrance (which is not easily effected without assistance or guidance) and then to the deepest possible penetration, which is best aided by encircling the central anatomy and making traction upon the buttocks.

The incentive to contact and penetration having been complied with to the limit of physical ability, an exaltation of sensation, or intensity of feeling, is produced by motion, which is of an undulatory or wave-like character and capable of being prolonged or retarded by voluntary effort.

Evidence of the senses comes from our habit of

constantly referring our sensations to external causes and upon our perception depends the reality of the external world.

Touch is simply exalted common sensation and depends upon the changes incident to contact with sensory nerves

There must be alterations of pressure contact if we are to perceive, and physical undulations most effectively bring the largest areas into varying contact and thereby cause the highest degree of bodily sensibility.

All parts of the body supplied with sensory nerves are organs of touch, yet some parts possess a far greater degree of delicacy (which may be much increased by practice) than others which are not so plentifully supplied with nerve endings.

Among the most sensitive parts are the tip of the tongue, the lips, the clitoris, the glans penis, the fingers, etc.

By a simultaneous bodily wavering, when coupling has been effected, there is pressure and friction upon some of the most sensitive areas and a little practice, together with anatomical knowledge, will enable a regulation of the sensation to suit the occasion.

Many women, for some reason or other, fail to help themselves to an orgasm, but with a little practice, co-operation and knowing how to do, a simultaneous climax may ordinarily be reached—without which copulation cannot be satisfactory, complete, or beneficial.

The question of how frequently to indulge in sexual refreshment is one which agitates the mind of nearly every one at some time during the married life.

Like any other exercise, a certain amount is unquestionably beneficial, but just what that amount is, it is very difficult if not impossible to state, and no fixed rules can be formulated that would strictly apply to even a majority of people at all times.

Very much depends upon the age, temperament, social conditions, habits of eating and drinking, climatic states, and especially previous sexual habits.

In the neighborhood of twenty years of age the person is capable of greater activity and all of his functions are susceptible to greater elasticity than is usually found a couple of decades later. Any exercise, including sexual, which would be readily borne and speedily recovered from in the earlier period might be excessive in later life.

Inclinations are to some extent transmitted by heredity, which makes some hardy and others less stable, and a certain amount of exertion would in one instance be tolerated and even strengthening, but might in another of opposite temperament be sufficient to cause fatigue and be injurious.

Conditions of life that render excitation more or less frequent, require periods of relaxation to counteract the excitability, if a happy medium is to be maintained. Sexual indulgence may be considered a sedative, but a frequency of intercourse under conditions that are recurrently exciting would be depressing if the influence of association did not create the demand.

A warm climate brings early maturity, and those who live where the temperature is high are more passionate and habitually indulge more freely than those who reside in a colder atmosphere, while the spring of the year is proverbially the time of love, as thoughts upon matters sexual vary with the changing seasons.

The needs of nutrition are imperative and surplus nutriment is readily utilized by sexual exercise.

Many of the bad effects that are usually attributed to sexual excesses could be more properly ascribed to high living.

Ordinary stimulants excite the sexual functions for the time being, but their prolonged use in large quantities reacts unfavorably and diminishes the sexual vigor.

Alcohol in small doses at first seems to increase sexual desire, and prostitution is most always associated with a free use of stimulants, for many of the follies which are committed with women are due to the effects of drinking.

Many resort to the use of whiskey, wine, etc., in order to revive their drooping courage and divert their thoughts into channels that lead to copulation, and the amount of intercourse being dependent upon the frequency of desire, it remains to be determined whether the bad effects of excesses are due to overindulgence in intercourse or the excessive use of stimulants.

High living certainly affects the frequency of sexual desire, and it would seem that the results of the fast lives led by people with "sporting" proclivities would primarily arise from the production of desire rather than from the gratification or relief of the same.

In practice it will be found that most always when

there is sexual excess it occurs either at times when the relations are illicit, or temporary, in which the utmost efforts are exerted to derive the greatest amount of pleasure within a limited time; or when the marital relation has been assumed after a life of continence.

Married people who confine their relations within the family, practically never, except there be a great difference in age or other extraordinary circumstances, indulge excessively in sexual intercourse after the novelty of the situation has worn away and they have become accustomed to each other.

On the contrary, it is more likely that under our social conditions more injury is wrought by irregular and denied relations than by the frequency of natural intercourse.

It is not so much the number of times that the act is practiced as it is the ardor with which it is undertaken and the thoroughness of its performance that is effective.

American men generally measure their sexual vigor and capacity by the number of times they are able to perform in one night and are wont to boast about the frequency of their ability; whereas some of the oriental males aim to remain in the vagina as long as possible (which is about fifteen minutes or upwards) and congratulate themselves upon the amount of pleasure they have been able to afford the woman.

The gallantry of many men would be much more appreciated and be prolific of far better results were they to imitate the conduct of those in the antipodes and follow their methods in the discharge of this family duty.

To the loss of sleep, which is more or less great at such times when sexual excesses are committed, should be attributed its due share when the depressing effects following in the wake of venereal orgies are considered.

Copulation is generally conducive to refreshing sleep when indulged in moderately, but the prevailing disposition to test the ability and take advantage of and make the most of secured opportunities that have been diligently sought with more or less sacrifices; together with the taking of stimulants that are sexually exciting, robs the person of timely sleep and causes a strain that is subsequently depressing and that requires additional recuperation, which, however, is impeded by the overexertion.

The effects of excessive sexual indulgence are, like those of masturbation, but temporary when the person is ordinarily healthy, and are recovered from quite as readily and speedily as from those of any other violent exercise or dissipation.

Unfortunately it is nearly always those persons who are by heredity more or less unstable that go to extremes in this, as in other directions. They are relatively poorly equipped to overcome emergencies, and in this event when prolonged sexual excesses are added to other extremes of conduct there may be disastrous results, but too frequent sexual indulgences are in themselves not nearly so injurious to normal people as to warrant what seems to be the popular belief.

Previous sexual habits determine to a great extent the amount of intercourse that is well borne.

Those who have been accustomed to sexual excitement and exercise of the genital organs, whether by manipulation or otherwise, do not become constitutionally affected like those who are not so familiar with the workings of their genitalia.

A man who has experienced orgasm many times has sexual organs that are not only well developed and functionally active, but are capable of a greater amount of exercise than the organs of one in whom the tissues are not accustomed to activity and have not been strengthened by use.

The mental power and capacity is often great in a person whose physical strength is limited, but it is the result of previous exercise and training and has been gradually developed.

The muscular development of an athlete enables him to perform feats that another person of equal size would not be capable of, and what would be exhilarating exercise for the one would prove very fatiguing for the other, who would suffer from overexertion.

Some persons who are strong in mind and body may be comparatively weak sexually, and it sometimes happens that consumptives, or those who are otherwise defective, manifest strong sexual powers.

To be able to perform any function well requires continued practice, and every prolonged intermission of exercise detracts from ability .

This holds good in sexual matters as well as in any other capacity.

The sexual organs of both men and women acquire greater capacity by their repeated hyperæmic conditions, and their sexual powers become increased by an exercise that is moderate and regular.

Some men who become fearful of declining vigor seek to conserve their power by abstaining from or diminishing the frequency of their accustomed regular relations, with the belief that they are endowed with a definite amount of sexual power and when that has been expended they will be left entirely without strength or desire.

A proficiency in any other capacity is acquired, maintained or increased only by continued practice, and it is not reasonable to suppose that an exception should be made of the sexual ability.

An athlete cannot remain strong and active without training; great minds are not acquired or retained unless they are worked; the ability to produce charming music, either vocal or instrumental, requires constant practice, and whatever dexterity has been attained needs application for its retention.

Nature has been very lavish in supplying the seed for propagation, for only an inconceivably small part of it finds conditions favorable for its growth.

The number of spermatozoa in a seminal emission varies somewhat with the frequency of ejaculation, but each emission contains millions, though only one is necessary for fructification.

The number found in an ordinary emission of about two drachms of seminal fluid is variously given from 30 to 500 millions, depending somewhat upon the time that has elapsed since the previous ejaculation (Sturgis.) The amount and consistency of the seminal fluid is influenced, among other things, by the prostatic secretion.

The Graafian follicles in the human female ovary, from whence come the ova that are impregnated upon conception, are also very numerous, and Foulis estimates that at birth each human ovary contains not less than 30,000.

The ovum in the female is developed, matured and discharged, whether copulation takes place or not, and as only an occasional one out of this vast number is impregnated by the male element, which is many times more numerous, it is obvious that nature has supplied a practically unlimited amount of fructifying material and guarded against all possible loss; and so it becomes apparent that a saving or sparing use of the vital principle is wholly uncalled for and no fear of exhausting the supply need be entertained.

On the contrary, it is highly probable that only a portion of the inherent amount is ever elaborated and discharged, and, other things being equal, the more that is produced, the greater the capacity for production.

We find this to obtain throughout the whole of organic life, and it is not to be presumed that the highest organization—man—is an exception.

The histories of many middle-aged men confirm the belief and substantiate the statement that they become gradually strengthened after marriage by the regular exercise of their sexual function, and an observing woman remarked with a wisdom born of experience, that a certain man was "A fine fellow but no good for a companion because he wasn't with a women often enough."

Very much misery would be averted if this fact were more widely known and a philosophical view taken with the exercise of patience and judicious conduct.

First attempts at sexual intercourse are very rarely successful and entirely satisfactory.

This statement may appear paradoxical to some, but it is nevertheless not far from the truth, even though more or less successful efforts have been previously made with another.

There are often several and nearly always one or more circumstances that prevent the necessary confidence in themselves or each other—to say nothing about the timely physical responsiveness—without which the harmony so essential to complete coitus is wanting, and which is not usually felt in the beginning of the sexual relation.

It is but natural to attribute failure to the active party, and hence the male is held, not only by himself but by the female, to be responsible for the shortcoming. This consciousness, which is usually felt, reacts very unfavorably, as it is deemed a reflection upon manhood and causes apprehension and chagrin.

Young men are generally more audacious and conceited than those of maturer years, but it requires more egotism and self-reliance than many possess to completely overcome the mortification of conscious sexual failure, and if confidence is not restored by subsequent success very much concern is felt.

The first failure makes a second attempt more

difficult, and unless encouragement be given by the passive party and confidence inspired, there will in all probability be a repetition of the first effort, if some days have elapsed between the trials.

The victim will now be in a mental state to become an easy prey to charlatans, particularly if the attempts at intercourse have been illicit.

There is no occasion for alarm, however, as his has been the usual experience, and any young man may consider himself fortunate if he be wholly successful after ten or a dozen trials in performing the act without experienced assistance and undue preliminary activity on the part of his consort.

Failure to successfully copulate during the first weeks of married life, when the woman has retained her virginity up to the time of marriage, is perhaps the rule.

After repeated attempts, the husband may succeed in effecting a satisfactory entrance before ejaculation, but that does not constitute physiological copulation.

The exchange of endearments incident to the ordinary courtship will doubtless have caused many seminal emissions without any actual attempts at connection, and when the vagina has been successfully entered, coitus is too often considered to have been complete.

We often hear of couples who have lived together a year or more without there having been a mutual orgasm, and many do not even know that there is such a thing for woman.

It will be sufficient to state that any well-born

man who has sexual organs with erectile ability, has it within himself to copulate as frequently and effectively as need be for all purposes, provided only that he be given encouragement, opportunity and the necessary practice.

He may also safely rest with the assurance that no matter what his previous sexual habits may have been, he will find in his marriage bed that which by intelligence, gentleness, patience and unselfish practices, will certainly bring mutual happiness, together with mutual sexual pleasure; but he alone must determine the responsiveness, for the chords which he touches will vibrate with sweet harmony or send forth grating discords as he may elect, and in accordance with his own conduct.

It may be said of humanity that if it lives for any one purpose more than another, that purpose is sexual.

The bad effects of sexual excesses and so-called self-abuse have, for moral or other reasons been improperly estimated and, in view of the almost universal prevalence of artificial acts, have been very greatly magnified.

It may not be amiss to state further that an ordinary man is no more apt to permanently hurt himself sexually than he is to overwork his body or severely tax his mental strength.

There is quite as much liability to injury from over-eating as from sexual excess, while the chances for his becoming a drunkard are greater, for the abuse of alcohol is responsible for many more cases of actual suffering than could possibly result from any personal acts of a sexual nature that an ordinary man would be likely to commit.

Women are less liable to bad physical effects from frequent normal sexual congress than are men.

Prolonged single acts of coitus give the maximum amount of pleasure and relief to woman, and it is also recognized that when the act is repeated several times in succession there is often more intense pleasure and orgasm with each repetition.

Cases of incompatibility might be greatly relieved if a hint were taken from the above and, instead of attempting a single act, as is most often the case in the married, a repetition be undertaken after the shortest possible interval, when it will be found that intercourse will often prove very much more satisfactory.

Something may be learned by a scientific and philosophical view and study of the lives of those women whose conduct is not limited to acts within orthodox confines, that may serve to aid us in determining what is, and what is not, excessive sexual indulgence.

In any large city may be found on the avenue, in the theater or at the races, middle-aged women that attract more than passing notice by their vivacious manner, independent air, stylish attire and graceful carriage.

They rear no children and assume no cares or responsibilities that can possibly be shifted upon another, and are bent only upon having a good time.

They sleep in the forenoon, devote the afternoon to shopping or leisure and entertain after dark.

They eat liberally of the best, drink unsparingly, deny themselves no luxury and permit whoever will to pay their bills.

Their careless, nonchalant and self-satisfied demeanor betokens a worldly wisdom and a keen knowledge of human nature, while their self-assurance may be attributed to mingling with "men-about-town" and confidence in their own ability to entertain.

They always have a "lover," on whom they shower gifts with a lavish hand, though they may change companions nightly, and sometimes even hourly, and it is not to be presumed that they stop short of anything but complete satiation of sensual pleasures.

They study how to create desire, are fond of show, display and accentuate their physical charms and know the strength and force of the sexual passion.

Aside from generosity these women possess no commendable or ennobling virtues, but an impartial observer will see that they continue to live year after year upon the fat of the land and often retain a freshness and well-preserved physique that is worthy of a better cause.

They continue their reckless lives, with perhaps an occasional spasm of virtue, until forced to relinquish them by disease or age.

Considering their almost constant exposure to infection and their dissipated habits others than sexual, it is astonishing to note to what degree they develop and maintain their physical vigor and attraction, for its must be acknowledged that among them may be found some of the prettiest of women.

It is true that the average life of a "woman of

the half world" is very short, but such women nearly always start with some unbalance and abandon themselves to every kind of dissipation, while their physical exposures and social deprivations are very great.

Cases of longevity in the more frugal are sufficiently numerous, however, to attract our attention and lead us to reflect upon the results of exaggerated exercise of the sexual function.

Comparing the men who lead similar lives, and who are their constant companions, with these women, we find that though both live amidst the same surroundings and under similar conditions, yet the women supply, in addition to their "lovers," many other men with sexual refreshment.

It is not to be presumed that they are inactive in the part they play, for upon the exhibitions of ardor whether it be real or assumed, depends their success, and whatever else may be said, it will scarcely be maintained that they are affected much more disastrously (except from the dangers of infection) than the men with whom they live and who cohabit many times less frequently than they.

The women of easy virtue place their sexual organs in use, and it must be said not altogether unwillingly on an average of perhaps five or ten times as often as those who confine their relations to one man, and, from a medical standpoint, the lesson to be learned and the points to be observed are these:

First. Women tolerate a greater amount of sexual activity than do men.

Second. Sexual excesses, if indeed it may properly be said that there be such without local abnormality, are not due so much to the act itself, but rather to the conditions which create an abnormal frequency of excitement.

This leads to the conclusion that it is probably not the sexual act which primarily may be injurious, but the frequent excitations that may become harmful, and which should be withheld or removed, and not the act proper avoided to prevent bodily harm.

When a comprehensive view of the entire question is taken and the situation considered in its various aspects, it will be found that it is quite as difficult to tell what the proper amount of sexual indulgence should be, as it is to determine the quantity of food to be eaten, to stipulate the measure of liquids to be consumed or to designate to what extent mental and physical exercise should be taken.

Each person should be governed by their own appetite or want, and guided by their conditions in this, as in other habits.

Ordinarily people partake of three meals daily, but many eat with greater frequency, and those who have been married a few years and are somewhere in the neighborhood of thirty-five years of age probably attempt to refresh themselves sexually on an average of two or three times weekly, when conditions are deemed favorable, with more or less success.

When younger or first married this amount is usually considerably increased, and as the years roll by it is gradually decreased until perhaps between fifty-five and sixty-five, when the sexual function in the male generally ceases to be noticeably active.

Owing to the prevailing sentiment that it is

unwomanly for the female to be actively solicitous and demonstrative in initiating, and unduly aggressive during the preliminaries to the act, the frequency of congress depends more largely upon the male, and the above statement permits of great variation within normal limits.

In one case almost daily depletion of the sexual organs is consistent with well-being, while in another of the same family one to three thorough sexual activities monthly seems adequate.

Many cases might be cited to show what the usual habits of people who live under the ordinary social conditions are, but the above will suffice to prove that sexual exercise is as various as any other, and may serve as a guide for the adjustment of individual cases.

The range is so wide within normal limits that little concern need be felt regarding excesses, provided only that the habits are regular and prolonged and the sexual life not subjected to abrupt changes, to which may be attributed any untoward effects.

Women especially run but little risks of injuring their health and happiness by excessive sexual practice that is legitimate and performed in the natural manner, for when the physical and mental condition is within normal limits and no undue stimulation resorted to, excess is highly improbable, if indeed it be possible.

There can be no doubt that the influence of prolonged continence upon either the male or female is to dwarf and in many respects destroy that which goes to make a broad and full physical and intellectual personality, and that to perform the sexual act whenever there is an existing state of sexual excitement, with the usual marital restrictions, is rather beneficial than otherwise.

CHAPTER IX

SEXUAL INEQUALITY

How Unequal Sexual States are Evolved—In Daily Life Honor Means Integrity for the Man and Chastity for the Woman—The Varying Effects of Discipline—Different Conditions of Married Women—A Wife Cannot Blame Others for Ignoring Her Humanity when She Forgets it —Advice Negative and no Instruction upon what is Most Vital—Women who can Always Respond to Husband the Happiest—Wives who are able to Help Themselves to an Orgasm—Those who are Dissatisfied with their Sexual Relations—Fifteen per cent. of Women are Practically Sexless—To Deprive a Wife of the most Profound Feelings Instilled by Life is to Deny a Created Being its Birthright—Bodily Contact Necessary for Excitement in Average Woman—The Requisites for Copulation are Desire, and Removal of Restrictions—Male Never Alarmed by Sexual Capability—Normal Coitus first Indication of Married Life—Desire Established by Acts that Cautiously Gravitate to Center—Man's duty to Elicit Response and Retard Orgasm—Wifely Obligations—Passion and Pregnancy—Women Reach Climax Against their Will—By Attention to Genital Congestion, Desire for Relief is Made Imperative—Suggestion in Cases of Delayed Practice—Analogy of Frigidity to Dyspepsia—By Giving that which Satisfies Manhood, Woman brings upon Herself Health and an Amiable Disposition—Combative Attitude—Silent Acquiescence and Active Response—No Submission in Absence of Emotion—Elimination of Fear—Climax Should be Sought when Intercourse is Attempted—Discreet Avoidance of Derogatory Remarks—With Knowledge and use of Tact, any Young Wife may Make her Relations to her own Liking.

That very much incompatibility exists in domestic life is recurrently emphasized and that the larger part of this distressing discord is primarily due to unequal sexual promptings and pleasures, becomes evident when a careful study of the two persons directly involved is made.

The underlying causes of incompatibility, or sexual inefficiency, are evolutional in their nature—that is to say, that the conditions are evolved or developed by the process of modern life.

The two sexes do not start equally in their development, and the conditions under which development progresses are vastly different in the two sexes.

The girl inherits a disposition to disregard matters of sex, and whatever propensity there may be to investigate the subject, is discouraged by association, for women generally do not discuss this topic and allude to it only with indefinite insinuations.

Young men and boys talk of these matters more freely and tell many stories that are woven about the sexual relation, though the truth is often perverted and very seldom told in its entirety.

Thought takes precedence of and greatly controls all physical processes and conditions.

When the attention is drawn to certain acts or things, the organs which perform the function suggested take on activity and a personal longing is incited.

To illustrate: The sight of something known to be good to eat awakens an appetite that would not otherwise prevail; the hearing of martial music inspires patriotism and moves one to keep time; the reading of a thermometer on a cold morning calls attention to the frigid atmosphere and makes one shiver; the detection of an abrasion makes one feel the slight wound, and the mental concentration upon any part of the body may, by its prolongation, be the cause of such constant and pronounced physiological activtity as to make the condition a pathological one.

Social conditions are such that the thoughts of the boy and youth are recurrently attracted to sexual matters, while those of the girl and maiden are diverted into other channels, which causes the development of the sexual system, as well as the sex feeling, to be smothered or retarded in the female, but to be stimulated and enhanced in the male.

Conscience, or that faculty which decides on the lawfulness or unlawfulness of our actions and affections, is very largely the result of teaching and has its influence in the production of sexuality.

Aside from a tendency that has been inherited, humanity is born without a conscience, and individuals soon acquire a varying capacity for its development.

Associations and moral influences create a sense of honor, which is an excellence of character, and practically means, in our daily life, integrity for the man and chastity for the woman.

Good breeding seeks to impress upon the girl that thoughts upon matters sexual are degrading, and since honor to her is a synonym of chastity, she avoids these thoughts as much as possible and does not jeopardize herself by discussing the topic, with the result that her sexual knowledge is comparatively rudimentary.

As the conscience is governed by the sense of honor and right, we find that what is priceless for the girl is of less practical value to the boy and he is therefore less restricted in his animal tendencies.

The very first discipline to which the boy is subjected, and the first duty impressed upon his primitive mind has for its object cleanliness, and he is instructed to make known his necessity for answering the repeated calls of nature.

After many chastisements he eventually learns to attend to his necessities by himself and, in order to evacuate bis bladder properly, he must handle his urinary, which is also his copulative organ. He is called upon to do this several times daily and very naturally retracts his foreskin many times.

Sooner or later, before the time of manhood, he will have experienced what results from successive retractions of the foreskin, and know, perchance, the feelings and conditions of sexual excitement, for it is not likely that he will require any specific instructions about the production of that exciting sensation to which he is by nature predisposed, though he will, by his association with other boys, not be lacking in opportunities for learning if he be less precocious than they.

His moral training leads him to throw the shroud of secrecy about his sexuality, and after puberty his manhood seeks to guard his organs from exposure, when occasion permits, to those who are not his intimates by the ever-present hand.

Oft repeated willful actions tend to become involuntary, and the hand readily gravitates to the genitalia when disrobed, and so the tranquility of the male sexual apparatus is disturbed with little provocation and its functional activity is consequently promoted.

At the marriageable age it will be found that the sexual sense has been developed to such a degree in the average male that it often requires but a thought, a look or a touch for sexual excitement, and but little more for a seminal ejaculation.

The ideal young woman would, if the usual admonitions were followed, be almost necessarily impotent at the time of her marriage, and without any disparagement it might be said that it is rather more fortunate than otherwise, when conjugal felicity is considered, that the ideal is not more often approached.

The female urinary apparatus requires no manual manipulation for the proper voiding of its excretion and the girl's necessities in this respect are complied with without touching the parts.

There is no conspicuous appendage to attract attention or curiosity, and the clothing is such that there are no pockets which make it convenient for the girl to touch or handle herself without detection.

Boyish habits, such as climbing, riding astride, etc., which may cause undue friction of the parts, are early interdicted, and it is not customary for girls to congregate and repair to a swimming hole where all clothing is dispensed with, bodies compared, abilities tested, and frolics engaged in which give so much pleasure to the average boy and afford opportunities for mutual investigations.

Personal inspection of the parts is very limited and more than casual glances of another is not so common, and, on the whole, the girl is not placed amidst conditions which would, in comparison, at all readily lead to functional activity of the sexual apparatus by mechanical means, as is the boy.

In the course of events the girl is not nearly so apt to discover by herself what causes the peculiar sensation of sexual excitation, and the chances of learning from another are also small when compared to those of the boy.

After maturity her conscience will have become very acute where sex is involved, and her scruples will be many.

If the sexual organs of the average young woman who has been carefully reared and who has passed her twenty-fifth year without marriage, be examined, it may be found that her clitoris is often small, rudimentary and scarcely to be felt; her labia thin, pale and undeveloped, with the vagina contracted, comparatively cool and dry, and the whole genitalia obtusely responsive.

With her there has been no occasion for recurrent functional activity of the sex organs, which is the average young man's daily experience and which forces the mind to think and dwell upon this primal function, while her precepts have been such as to prompt a smothering and misinterpretation of inherited animal tendencies.

The natural love of praise, which has been accentuated by frequent laudation, makes her think much of those little acts of endearment which serve as preliminaries to copulation, but her thoughts habitually stop short of considering the act itself, which to her is depicted as shocking and to be avoided.

The following narrative, written by a married lady

and found in a recent work upon sexual matters, is so well written that we cannot do better than to reproduce it here in her own language. She describes her life as a child, gives her girlish sentiments and analyzes her emotions with these words:

"My mother (herself a very passionate and attractive woman) recognized the difficulty for English girls of getting satisfactorily married, and determined if possible to shield us from disappointment by turning our thoughts in a different direction. Theoretically the idea was perhaps good, but in practice it proved useless. The natural desires were there. Disappointment and disillusion followed their repression none the less surely for having altered their natural shape. I think the love I had for my mother was almost sexual, as to be with her was a keen pleasure, and to be long away from her an almost unendurable pain. She used to talk to us a good deal on all sorts of subjects, but she never troubled about education in the ordinary sense. When nine years old I had been taught nothing except to read and write. She never forbade us to read anything, but if by accident we got hold of a book of which she did not approve, she used to say: 'I think that is rather a silly story, don't you?' We were so eager to come up to her standard of taste that we at once imagined we thought it silly, too. In the same way she discouraged ideas about love or marriage, not by suggesting there was anything wrong or improper about them, but by implying great contempt for girls who thought about lovers, etc.

"Up to the age of twenty I had a vague general impression that love was very well for ordinary women, but far beneath the dignity of a somewhat superior person like myself. To show how little it entered my thoughts I may add that, up to seventeen I fancied a woman got a child by being kissed on the lips by a man. Hence all the fuss in novels about the kiss on the mouth. When I was nine years old I began to feel a great craving for scientific knowledge. A 'Child's Guide to Science,' which I discovered at a second hand book-stall (and which, by the way, informed me that heat is due to a substance called caloric), became a constant companion. In order to learn about light and gravitation, I saved up my money and ordered (of all books) Newton's Principia, shedding bitter tears when I found I could not understand a word of it. At the time I was horribly ashamed of this desire for knowledge. I got such books as I could surreptitiously and hid them in odd corners. Why, I cannot imagine, as no one would have objected, but, on the contrary, I should have been helped to suitable books. My sisters and I were all violently argumentative, but our quarrels were all on abstract subjects. We saw little of other children and made no friendships, preferring each other's society to that of outsiders. When I was about ten a girl of the same age come to stay with us for a few days. When we went to bed the first night she asked me if I ever played with myself, whereupon I took a great dislike to her. No sexual ideas or feelings were excited. When still quite a child, however, I had feelings of excitement which I now recognize as sexual. Such feelings always came to me in bed (at least I cannot remember them at any other time) and were generally accompanied by a gradually increasing desire to make water. For a long time I would not get out of bed for fear of being scolded for staying awake, and only did so at last when actually compelled. In the meantime the sexual excitement increased also, and I believe I thought the latter was the result of the former, or perhaps rather, that both were the same thing. (This was when I was about seven or eight years old.) So far as I can recollect, the excitement did not recur when the desire to make water had been gratified. I seemed to remember wondering why thinking of certain things (I can't remember what these were) should make one want to urinate. (In later life I have found that if the bladder is not emptied before coitus, pleasure is often more intense.) There were also feelings, which I now recognize as sexual, in connection with ideas of whipping. * * *At fourteen I went to a boarding school, where there were seventy girls between the ages of seven and nineteen. I think it goes to show that there is but very little sexual precocity among English girls that during the three years I stayed there I never heard a word the strictest mother would have objected to. One or two of the older girls were occasionally a little sentimental, but on no occasion did I hear the physical side of things touched upon. I think this is partly due to the amount of exercise we took. When picturing my childhood I always see myself racing about, jumping walls, climbing trees. In France and Italy I have been struck by the greater sedateness of Continental children. Our idea of naughtiness consisted chiefly in having suppers in our bedrooms and sliding down the banisters after being sent to bed. The first gratified our natural appetite, while the second supplied the necessary thrill in the fear of being caught. I made no violent friendships with the other girls, but I became much attached to the French governess. She was thirty and a born teacher, very strict with all of us, and doubly so with me for fear of showing favoritism. But she was never unjust, and I was rather proud of her severity and took a certain pleasure in being punished by her, the punishment always taking the form of learning by heart, which I rather liked doing. So I had my thrill, excitement, I don't know what to call it, without any very great inconvenience to myself.

"Just before we left school the sexual instinct began to show itself in enthusiasm for art with a capital A, Ouida's novels being mainly responsible. My sister and I agreed that we would spend our lives traveling about France, Italy and the Continent, with a violin in one pocket and an Atravante Dante in the other. To do this satisfactorily to ourselves we must be artists, and I resolved to go in for music and become a second Liszt. When my father offered to take us to Italy, the artist's mecca, for a couple of years, we were wild with delight. We went, and disillusionment began. It may perhaps seem absurd, but we suffered acutely that first summer. Our villa was quite on the beach, the lowest of its flight of steps being washed by the Mediterranean. At the back were grounds which seemed a paradise. Long alleys covered over with vines and carpeted with long grass and poppies, grassy slopes dotted with olives and ilex, roses everywhere, and almost every flower in profusion, with, at night, the fire-flies and the heavy scents of syringa and orange blossoms. In the midst of every possible excitement to the senses there was one thing wanting, and we did not know what that was. We attributed our restlessness and dissatisfaction to the slow progress in our artistic education, and consoled ourselves by thinking when we once had mastered the technical difficulties we should feel all right. And of course we did derive a very real pleasure from all the beauties of art and nature with which Italy abounds. It seems to me now, however, that the art craze is one of the modern phases of woman's sexual life. When we were in Italy the great centers of the country were overrun with girls studying art, most of whom had very little talent, but who had mistaken the restlessness due to the first awakening of the sexual instinct for the divine flame of genius. In our case it did not matter, as we were not dependent upon our own exertions. But it must have been terribly hard for girls who had burned their boats and chosen art as a career, to have added to the repression of their natural desires the bitterness of knowing that in their chosen walk of life they were failures. The results as far as work goes might not be so bad if the passions, as in men, were occasionally gratified. It is the constant drudgery, combined with the disappointment and finding that art alone does not satisfy which is so paralyzing. Besides, sexual gratification is always followed by exaltation of the mental faculties with, in my experience, no depressing reaction such as follows pleasure excited by mental casues alone. At one time when living at the villa I met a man about forty-five, who took rather a fancy to me. I mention this because it woke me up; no emotion was excited, but I realized for the first time (I must have been nearly twenty) that I was no longer a child, and that a man could think of me in connection with love. It was only after this, and not immediately after, either, that men's society began to have an interest for me, and that I began to think a man's love would be a pleasant thing to possess, after all. The sexual instinct, at any rate as regards consciousness, thus developed slowly and in what I believe to be a very usual sequence; religion, admiration for an older woman, and art. I am not sure that I have made quite enough of the first, yet I do not know that there is any more to say. There were very strong physical feelings connected with all these which were identical with those now connected with passion, but they were completely satisfied by the mental idea which excited them. The first time I can remember feeling keen pleasure was when I was between seven and eight years old. I can't recollect the cause, but I remember lying quite still in my little cot clasping the iron rails at the top. It may be said that this is hardly slow development, but I mean slow as regards (1) any connection of the idea with a man or (2) any physical means of excitation.

"I have laid stress on my desire for knowledge, as I think my sexual feelings were affected by it. A great part of my feeling for my mother was due to the stores of information she appeared to possess. * * * My French teacher's capacity was her chief attraction. When, as a girl, I thought of marriage, I desired a man that could 'explain things to me.' One learns later to live one's mental and sexual life separately to a great extent. But at twenty I could not have done so; given the opportunity I should have made the mistake of Dorothea in Middlemarch. I have spoken of the depressing after-effects of pleasure brought about by a purely mental cause, but I do not think this is the case in childhood and early youth. (Perhaps some women feel no such depression afterward, and this may account for their coldness in regard to men.) This may perhaps be accounted for by the fact that it occurs much more rarely, and also it is perhaps a natural process before the sexual organs fully develop, and so not harmful.

"I always find it difficult in expressing the different degrees of physcial excitement even to myself, though I know exactly what I felt. As a child, from the time of the early experiencc already mentioned (about the age of seven or eight) and as a young girl, the second stage (secretion of mucus) was already reached. The amount of secretion has always been excessive, but at first secretion only lasted a short time; later it began to last for several hours, or even sometimes the whole night, if the natural gratification has been withheld for a long time(say, three months). I do not remember ever feeling the third stage (complete orgasm) until I saw the first man I fancied I cared for. I do not think that mental causes alone have ever produced more than the first two stages (general diffuse excitement and secretion). I have sometimes wondered whether I could produce the third mechanically, but I have a curious unreasonable repugnance to trying the experiment; it would seem to materialize it too much. As a child and a girl I was contented to arrive at the second stage, possibly because I did not realize that there was any other, and perhaps this is why I have experienced no evil results. In dreams the third stage seems to come suddenly without any leading up to it, either mental or physical, of which I am conscious. I do not, however, remember having such dreams before I was engaged. They came at a later period; even then when great pleasure was experienced, it came, as a rule, suddenly and sharply, with no dreams leading up to it. The dreams generally take a sad form (an Evangeline and Gabriel business, where one vainly seeks the person who eludes one). I have, however, sometimes had pleasurable dreams of men who were quite indifferent to me and of whom I never thought when awake. The impression on awakening is so strong one could almost fancy one's self really in love with them. I can quite understand falling in love with a person by dreaming of them in this way.

"The first time I can remember experiencing the third stage in waking moments was at a picnic, when the man to whom I have before referred as the first that I fancied that I cared for, leaned against me accidentally in passing a plate or dish; but I was already in a violent state of excitement at being with him. There was no possibility of anything between us, as he was married. If he guessed my feelings, they were never admitted, as I did my best to hide them. I never experienced this, except at the touch of some one I loved. (I think the saying about the woman 'desiring the desire of the man' is just about as true as most epigrams. It is the man's personality alone which affects me. His feelings toward me are of—I was going to say indifference, but at any rate quite secondary importance, and the gratification of my own vanity counts as nothing in such relations.) As a rule to reach even the second stage, the exciting ideas must be associated with some particular person, except in the case of a story, where one identifies one's self with one of the characters. * * * In the case of my governess, my feelings were aroused in exactly the same way as later they would be by one's lover. In the art craze I am rather vague as to how it came about, but I think, as a rule, there was rather a craving for pleasure than pleasure itself. I do not remember ever thinking much about the physical feeling. It seemed as natural that a pleasant emotion should produce pleasant physical effects as that a painful one should cause tears. As a child one takes so much for granted.

"I may summarize my own feelings thus: First exciting ideas alone produce, as a rule, merely the first stage of sexual excitement. Second, the same ideas connected with a particular person will produce the second stage. Third, the same may be said of the presence of the beloved one. Fourth, actual contact appears necessary for the third stage. If the first stage only be reached, the sensation is not pleasurable, in reality, or would not be but for its associations. If produced, as I have sometimes found it to be, by a sense of mental incapacity, it is distinctly disagreeable, especially if one feels that the energy which might have been used in coping with the difficulty is being thus dissipated. If it be produced, as it may be, as the result of physical or mental restraint, it is also unpleasant unless the restraint were put upon one by a person one loves. Then, however, the second stage would probably be reached, but this would depend a good deal on one's mood. If the first stage only were reached, I think it would be disagreeable; it would be a conflict between one's will and sexual feeling. Perhaps women who feel actual repugnance to the sexual act with a man they love have never gone beyond the first stage, when their dislike to it would be quite intelligible to me."

The conditions by which sentiment is evolved and physical states developed are so widely different that we find at the time of marriage a great variance in the sexual status, which makes the principals very unequal in sexual capacity, but which must needs be developed into greater equality if harmonious relations are to be secured and maintained.

Briefly stated, we have at this period for companions, on the one hand, a man with a highly developed sexual sense of several years' duration; a mind cognizant of sexuality; generative organs accustomed to functional activity, with an intimate relation between the two that makes them greatly influential, acutely sensitive and readily responsive each to the other; but who has little understanding of femininity and less knowledge of sexual hygiene.

On the other hand, a woman whose previous education and environment precluded a proper understanding of sexuality; who does not recognize the origin of, nor properly interpret her feelings; whose sexual organs are comparatively rudimentary and incapable of timely activity; who has many misgivings and seeks to avoid that which would prove most beneficial, but invites and tolerates such acts as cause great perturbation and excitement without affording proper relief.

With these conditions—and they are the usual ones—it is practically impossible to obtain the full physiological or beneficial effects of intercourse in the beginning, and if these are not eventually experienced, indifference, disgust or repugnance takes the place of what should be connubial bliss.

If the sexual relations in the home were satisfactory and all that could be desired, it is not at all probable that there would be illicit relations, as there would be no temptation to seek what had already been found

If the sexual act at all times gave pleasure to both husband and wife it would be sought for mutual happiness, and unless such is the case harmonious relations, upon which the efficacy of the act depends, cannot exist.

For the man there must be some little pleasure or the act cannot take place at all, though the frequency with which the act is attempted and the satisfaction derived depends largely upon the woman.

The conditions of women in regard to their marital relations vary with the individual, and for convenience married women have been divided into the following classes:

First. Women so situated and constructed, both physically and mentally, that they respond to the caresses of the husband at all times.

Second. Those who can under reasonable circumstances, by a voluntary effort hasten or retard the climax to meet the varying conditions under which they live.

Third. Those who are unable to properly participate, or bring into requisition any physical or mental methods to produce simultaneous orgasm, or harmonious relations, but are left excited, nervous and unsatisfied after coition.

Fourth. Women whose sexual passion does not become aroused; who do not derive any pleasure or benefit from copulation, and who cannot conceive how the act can be pleasurable for anyone.

This division is somewhat arbitrary, as it is possible for a woman to be put in any of these classes at different times during her marital life.

It is also impossible to determine the proportion of women in any of these classes, but it has been estimated that the first class embraces 5 per cent.; the second, 50 per cent.; the third, 30 per cent., and the last 15 per cent. of all married women.

According to this estimate nearly one-half the women are living lives that can be neither healthful nor congenial, and whose homes are lacking in a fundamental requisite for happiness.

Not only is the woman concerned, but the remainder of the family is directly involved, and when we consider the prevalence of these undesirable conditions the situation becomes appalling.

Granting for the sake of argument, that the proportion of congenial homes is larger than that given, it is still a wonder, not that divorce is so common, but rather that it is not obtained with greater frequency.

In order to mitigate the evil it becomes necessary to remove the cause, and fine theories, however brilliantly promulgated, are of but little avail if practical results are not forthcoming.

Since biblical times the masculine portion of humanity at least, has been accustomed to frequent sexual intercourse, and this predisposition has been transmitted from father to son through countless generations; and inasmuch as man has had this habit since the time of recorded history, unless human nature greatly changes—of which there is no hope—he will continue so inclined.

That sexual inequality is the cause of much ill-health and a great deal of misery goes without saying, and any work which conduces to greater equality and makes humanity better, more peaceful and happy, is the true philanthropy and should be hailed with delight and encouraged.

We should always keep in mind that absolute perfection is not of this world. The ideal married state is one in which both the husband and wife desire the same thing at the same time, and each possesses the ability and does satisfy the want of the other.

Harmony in domestic relations is of the greatest importance, and if the husband's acts appear selfishly brutal, or the wife forgets that she is a woman, all hope of amicable relations must be lost.

When a woman at all times assumes an angelic attitude in bed, her health is endangered and her earthly happiness has "gone glimmering," for she cannot justly blame others for ignoring her humanity when she herself persistently fails to display it.

The eternal fitness of things prevents drawing-room conduct from necessarily being at all times the best of bed manners, and the sooner people are taught to realize and act humanely, the less often will proprieties be violated, and humanity will be thereby benefited.

If the laity knew what the proper sexual relations were, much harm would be averted, but it is not enough to know what this condition is, for it requires specific instructions to bring about this end.

The physician, even, must not only know what is required, but it is his duty to so instruct his patients that they may accomplish what is essential.

There is no doubt but that, if both parties knew what was required for their welfare and had within themselves the ability to carry out what is necessary they would eagerly strive to attain that which would be to their personal benefit.

Without the danger of a challenge, it may be asserted that with proper and timely education on matters sexual, there is no good reason why any sexual relations that are at all usual could not be made most satisfactory for all concerned, and that this would obtain if people only knew how, is philosophical and not visionary.

The women belonging to the first class heretofore enumerated, or those who always respond to the caresses of the husband and have natural coitus, are the best of companions.

They are bright, brilliant and vivacious, have cultivated intuitions that anticipate pleasurable relations.

and both take and give delight readily. They are happy in their love, elicit attentions, often obtain distinction, and, when discreet, are the happiest of women.

That the proportion of such wives is not larger is unfortunate, but that many more could be in the same position there is every reason for belief.

The condition is the result of extraordinary affinity, exceptional knowledge of sexuality and human nature, early marriage and long familiarity with sexual practices.

This class needs no medical advice or encouragement in their relations.

In the second class, in which one-half of the women are placed, are those who are capable of adjusting themselves to ordinary conditions and have physiological copulation when they choose.

They are comparatively contented and silent, deeming their relations sacred and not to be alluded to.

They make devoted wives, adorable mothers and true helpmates; command respect, receive consideration and live for their homes, husbands and children They are loyal in adversity, joyful in prosperity, and admirable wherever placed.

They meet their husbands half way, uncomplainingly; are the source of ennobling inspirations, call forth tender feelings and leave behind an honored memory.

With them there is no infidelity; they wield the greatest influence, and when unmolested are altogether honored and lovable, within and without the family

The family is their greatest concern, and were it not for the manifold temptations of our society that prompt to its restriction, there would remain but little to be desired for the happiest sexual living.

The women of the third class, or those who are unable to bring themselves to the point where there will be eager participation in the pleasures of sexual intercourse, are in considerable numbers, as the proportion is estimated at 30 per cent.

They do not satisfy their husbands, except in some minor degree, neither are their husbands considered by them very acceptable.

Both are dissatisfied with their relations and seek to promote their happiness by methods other than the right.

Their temptation to derive pleasures of sense elsewhere than from the prescribed source, is in proportion to their personal makeup, and their conduct depends largely upon their opportunities and the people with whom they come in contact.

Very often they find a paramour with whom they temporarily enjoy, for a varying length of time, those pleasures they should have in their relations at home and if they be successful in disguising their duplicity —which is most often the case—the world remains ignorant of the real condition.

Not content at home they woo excitement and diversion in the various and numerous methods at their command and partially console themselves with the belief that they are enjoying themselves.

If daring enough to brave society's comments, they sometimes, especially when a more congenial alliance seems in prospect, enter the courts and pray for divorce and thus proclaim and establish the fact that their marriage is a failure.

These are the cases that require advice, as most of the trouble originates in ignorance and the mystery with which sex is popularly surrounded.

The wife does not know how to obtain the satisfaction and tranquility that is needed, and the husband does not understand how to impart and obtain that which must necessarily draw the two closer together and cement the bonds.

Much can be accomplished by proper instruction, and if the case has not already gone on to that stage where a hopeless infatuation has been formed for another, the condition can often be remedied by effective personal acts alone, and nearly always rectified by local measures which put the woman in the way of securing the results that are indispensable to right sexual living, and so essential for adult humanity's welfare.

Women of the last class, who are devoid of sexual feeling, or passion, are in need of sympathy.

These women are practically sexless, and that 15 per cent, or one woman in every seven, is living her life with nothing but childish or senile sentiments and intuitions, is no credit to our boasted civilization with its much vaunted facilities for education—that does not include the learning of the vital principles of right living.

That women should be called upon to bear and rear children without taking any interest in, or actively participating in that process which is necessary for their origin, is manifestly cruel, unjust and inhuman.

To prevent or deprive a similar being from having the most profound feelings instilled by life, and which go with the manner of imparting this being to another, is to deny a created entity its birthright, to put it mildly.

It is difficult, if not impossible, for a person to understand a sensation they have never experienced and of which they have no personal knowledge, and so these women cannot conceive how there can be any pleasure in this act, which is frequently referred to as base and degrading.

They experience no more sensation or pleasure than from ordinary close contact, and submit from a sense of wifely duty, or a desire to please the husband, who is known to have animal necessities, which are often termed "beastly" tendencies.

They become pregnant and rear families to whom they are quite as devoted as the women who have natural feelings.

Any allusions to benefits derived from copulation or to others of their sex who enjoy it, meet with their emphatic contempt, and they persistently endeavor to influence all whom they may with their ideas.

They are most severe in condemnation of erring women, are sometimes insanely jealous, and more or less warped in their judgment.

Their solicitude for other women is often marked, but misplaced, for they themselves, as well as their husbands, are truly deserving of compassion.

Advice in these cases is thrown away and argument is useless, for unless they are personally brought to feel that which is unknown to them, they will remain serenely unconscious of the natural sexual feelings, which have such a tremendous influence upon the affairs of life.

If they have been married a number of years, any instructions which may be given them relative to the requisites for copulation will prove inadequate, as their mental attitude prohibits the required mood for enjoyment, and unless extraordinary means can be resorted to whereby the local physical condition becomes sufficiently pronounced to dominate the mind, active participation and harmonious sexual relations cannot be had.

With the average female, not only is bodily contact necessary to produce sexual excitement, the greater part of the time, but a slowness of response and a limited area of physical excitability are the rule. Little acts that show affection, and ordinary caresses serve to establish a receptive mood, but very often contact with one or more of the sexual centers is necessary to produce the physical conditions that are required for normal congress.

Whenever anything is done that gives a feeling of well-being and affords pleasure in the doing, it requires no urging for a repetition, as it is safe to predict that it will be repeated as often as possible, if the opportunity is afforded and the ability for enjoyment is possessed.

There can be no greater human pleasures for adult men and women than those afforded by their sexual relations, when these are as nature designed, and if they were always satisfactory and never followed by undesirable results there would be nothing to hope for, other things being equal.

Given the ability to enjoy and the assurance of freedom from harmful results, the obstacles to the happiest possible sexual living would be removed.

These obstacles are in practice very formidable, however, for it is given to but very few to have them removed to such a degree as will be mutually satisfactory.

We are considering only married people before the age in which the change of life occurs or such a time when sexual desire naturally ceases to be active.

The two requisites in question are:

First. Proper frequency of desire, or ability to copulate.

Second. Removal of the restrictions placed upon the gratification of this desire.

Practically, gratification is denied or restricted by a solicitude regarding pregnancy, which also greatly affects desire.

Failure of issue may, possibly, by its general influence upon the two lives, have some effect upon sexuality, but nearly always the fear of pregnancy is the great and underlying cause which prevents desirable sexual relations.

Mutual preparation for the act is essential, and in this the husband is more largely concerned, while the fear of pregnancy prevents the wife from taking her proper part, as she is thereby more directly affected.

The ordinary man is not alarmed by his own sexual excitation, but is often greatly concerned about its absence.

His facilities for, and its proper gratification, are the source of his great solicitude; but so long as he awakens with physical evidence of his virility and possesses the consciousness of his ability to copulate he is satisfied with his personal sexuality.

In event of his being convinced that he is prematurely without sexual vigor, he chides himself with "lost manhood" and often exerts himself to regain it; but never is he dissatisfied with his sexual capacity, though he is usually worried about the practicability of his sexual acts.

When his "manhood" is unquestioned, it is the practice of his sexual function that commands the serious and secret consideration of the average husband, and in this he must have the co-operation of the wife.

His pleasure depends mostly upon the eagerness of the wife, and, if for no other reason, he should, therefore, study how to afford his companion the greatest enjoyment in their sexual relations.

Before marriage the momentous question is the establishment of relations, but after matrimony the problem to be solved is the proper conduct in the nuptial couch.

When, in sexual congress, the delights and benefits of a mutual orgasm have once been thoroughly experienced, the natural appetite prompts to subsequent solicitation, and it is quite as natural for a woman to seek the normal way of satisfying her passion with her husband as it is for her to want to quench her thirst by the drinking of cool water.

Remembering the varying conditions of life previous to marriage and the usual inequality at this time, the first aim should be to bring about normal coitus and then if the other great obstacle—undesirable results—be overcome, equal sexual ability will naturally develop very rapidly, with judicious conduct.

The sooner this is accomplished after the wedding the better.

That mutual orgasm is not experienced until a comparatively long time afterward, if at all, is due mostly to ignorance which must be charged to the aggressive party, as he is in the main at fault, if either is to be blamed.

No definite statement relative to the time required for the usual development of synchronous orgasm can be given, as no statistics are available, but it is often from several months to a couple of years, after which time it will be attained with more or less difficulty, when the husband and wife are left to themselves and no assistance rendered.

The average woman requires bodily contact for preparation, and it is the husband's duty to furnish this in a manner that will be effective.

Abrupt onslaught is detrimental and often fatal to progress, and so the sexual centers should be cautiously and gradually approached if an even start is to be obtained.

The male must first of all elicit response to his advances, and if only his presence be tolerated, this will sooner or later be forthcoming with the proper procedure.

By stimulation of the outlying zones, the great center of sexual excitement is reflexly converted into a condition that permits of its natural function, and a state of quiescence, or rest, is transformed into one of activity and physical fitness. These areas, zones or centers have been previously enumerated and repetition here would be superfluous.

Attention to these preliminaries, which are so essential and greatly appreciated by women, should never be neglected but should precede each and every sexual act, and prolonged until such a time as the genitalia may become distended and prepared.

The man's duty does not by any means end here, for the average woman is slower in reaching the climax than is her consort, as the complexity of her sexual mechanism is much greater.

As a rule it will be necessary for the man to retard, prolong or extend the second stage of the act (or the voluntary activity of coupling) as long as possible, or until the woman is in a condition to be relieved by the explosive power of an orgasm, with its profound sedative and tranquilizing effect.

The tendency of sensitive men is to rapid and premature arrival at the point of ejaculation, and when this stage is reached a cessation of activity is imperative.

In many cases it will be very difficult to retain sufficient control in the beginning of relations, but with persistent efforts it will, in most instances, be eventually obtained.

With a check upon the aggressor and encouraging progression in the party of the second part, there is no reason why sexual equality cannot be developed, and amicable, as well as beneficial, coitus be experienced.

Having prepared, by judicious handling, and with gradually progressive acts that cautiously gravitate to the great center of sexual attraction; and having by deliberation given reasonable time and opportunity for response, the husband will have discharged his every duty and have contributed what lies within his power to the most healthful and, therefore, happy sexual living.

The wife's obligations are perhaps more exacting but none the less essential for harmonious relations.

Her natural and apparently passive part must partake of the proper receptivity. "Reciprocity" should be her policy in the conduct of family affairs.

Having once been in the position to know and experience the delights and personal benefits, of physiological congress, it lies within her power and becomes her duty to so regulate the relations as to be mutually satisfactory and all that could be reasonably desired.

She it is who, by her conduct and manner, helps herself to the greatest womanly heritage, and in so doing gives to the husband that which no other woman can bestow, and against which no wiles are enticing, no charms alluring and no earthly power sufficiently great to completely or permanently destroy.

No man, however ennobled or depraved, but is made more tender and sympathetic by a quivering response to his masculine touch, and the animated thrill of a conscious and timely emotion during exalted feeling, is ever entrancing.

Woman's first actual sexual experience can not, for anatomical reasons, be altogether agreeable, but is most often more or less painful, and its memory not readily effaced.

The existent emotion will have received a sudden shock, but the actual injury is but slight and the discomfort temporary and overshadowed by subsequent desire, if due consideration be shown.

In some rare instances the hymen, which obstructs the vaginal entrance, is of such size and structure as to impede progress, but when once ruptured and healed, which it ordinarily very readily does, the subsequent acts are never painful when properly done and normal physical conditions prevail.

Cases are now and again encountered by physicians where a rigid hymen is found intact several months or even years after marriage, but these only emphasize the prevailing popular ignorance of sexual matters.

Until such a time when a woman really knows all that the sexual act affords, the bedroom etiquette of the pair, and the varying results, are very largely what the man makes them; but after this time, in everyday life, it is practically the woman who is most responsible for the congeniality of the sexual relations.

Some women will not discuss or reveal to their husbands their personal sexual status, but will confide to the physician many things which, if known to the husband and judiciously acted upon would very often be conducive to the couple's mutual benefit.

They may sometimes exchange ideas with other women (though this is done mostly with considerable reserve) but they cannot bring themselves to the point of conveying their thoughts to the husband, except by indirect references, which he is unable to correctly understand.

To a lover in whom there is no more interest than a temporary exchange of pleasures, will occasionally be revealed a condition which, if shown to the husband, would afford quite as much pleasure and be conducive to greater family unity and harmony.

The common belief that a show of passion to the husband will forfeit his respect and devotion, may keep some women from assisting themselves to an orgasm.

Though there may be some ground for this opinion, yet whatever a man may admire in a woman outside of marriage, when he is joined with one in wedlock, every sensible man appreciates a flesh and blood woman in his bed quite as much as at his table, and practically, wifely obligations are much more satisfactorily discharged by supplying sexual refreshment than by simply helping to deplete the family larder.

There is no woman who has not given pregnancy most serious consideration, and the anxieties of those who are in positions which render them susceptible to this state, are among the greatest.

Even after the time of having signified her willingness to assume the sexual relation, the average young wife of to-day requires to be satisfied with her chances of expectancy before she is in the proper mood for sexual congress.

She must feel a certain sense of security for the time being, or temporarily disregard this consequence if she is to play such a part as will render the act most successful.

When full cognizance of what the function affords in the way of pleasure is had, the risk may be ignored, but any dread must be relegated to the background if copulation is to be most complete.

The tremendous influence of created fear, which prospective parentage engenders, upon the relations in the earlier married life, is not always realized and can scarcely be overestimated.

Without a feeling of this responsibility, sexual equality would be speedily and instinctively developed after marriage, and the most pleasant of sexual relations obtain, except in the most extraordinary and very rare instances.

The cares and deprivations which the rearing of children entails means much to the father, but the personal discomfort or danger and the many exactions fall more heavily upon the mother, and as the love for individual children grows with their presence, the inconvenient coming of additional ones stands out in bold relief and causes such great apprehension that it cannot be ignored.

Those women who can, and sometimes do, assist in the act to the extent of helping themselves to the climax, would, when given reasonable assurance of immunity, always try to so conduct themselves as to bring about this desirable end.

That they are left unsatisfied and nervous after commerce is due to their own choosing between what is deemed to be to their greater or lesser discomfort.

Their preferred conduct would be to follow their natural inclination for the time being, but the conviction of possible ultimate complications is so overwhelming as to influence them to forego the immediate pleasure.

Like other absurd ideas that cluster about the copulative act, there is quite an extensive belief prevalent among women that if passion is suppressed the liability to conception is thereby greatly diminished or removed, and hence they are persistent in their efforts to subdue their feelings.

This opinion is, of course, entirely erroneous and without any foundation, but nevertheless women permit themselves to be governed by such a fallacy and jeopardize their best interests.

The very common practice of "withdrawal," to which the husband is often persuaded, reacts with the greater injury upon the woman.

If the woman permitted herself to act in accordance with her natural emotion at this time, the male could not readily withdraw at this critical period if he would, as her efforts at retention would serve as an impediment.

Aside from the mental effect of outraged manhood, which is always detrimental, the effect of this practice upon the man is inconsiderable when compared to the condition in which the woman is left.

The physical effect upon the man, if we except the additional strain of his struggle with the impulse, is much the same as that of normal contact, as the depleting effect of the emission will relieve the tension and have a sedative action, and, though the beneficial effects of natural coitus will not be obtained, yet the injury to the man will not be as great as that to the woman.

In addition to the disgust with which rebellious nature punishes a violation, the woman in this event is left unappeased and excited, with her genitalia congested, and with no spasmodic depletion to relieve the tension.

She will regain composure only after such a time as the circulation has become equalized, which is indefinite.

For her there has been no compensation whatever, her nervous system has been disturbed, her mind perverted, her sex abused and her temper severely ruffled.

She cannot be sure that the procedure has been prohibitive and she awaits her recurrent menstruation with misgivings.

Similar efforts only exaggerate her condition and eventually her mechanism is disturbed to an extent that makes harmonious action difficult and natural response to stimuli uncertain.

When oft-repeated she is more or less constantly in a state of unrest, or nervousness, and her genital organs may be in a mild state of chronic congestion.

She will probably develop some leucorrhœa and be predisposed to menstrual disorders.

Instead of developng equality the breach is widened and family relations become strained.

The hereditaments of primitive man are universally possessed, but society and the conventions of civilization make us ashamed to reveal ourselves and lead to the wearing of masks.

Women who cannot bring themselves to the point of active participation in congress, but who now and again experience an orgasm, do so in spite of themselves, as nature asserts itself without and against their own volition.

Under especially favorable circumstances, when by some means the impulse is exceptionally heightened or the sensibilities altered, attempts at connection will be met with a natural finish.

Instead of this being an occasion for rejoicing, it is looked upon with a reproachful spirit by these misguided women and a determination is conceived not to permit its subsequent occurrence.

With such, the proper procedure is to educate and persuade them to the rational way of thinking, and to frequently bring about those conditions when nature demands its sway and overcomes artificial impediments.

When the beneficial effects become apparent to such an extent as to induce conviction, the scruples will be overcome and the battle more than half won.

In the beginning of married life this will be much easier than later, when the prejudices have become more deeply and firmly rooted and less likely to be overcome.

Advantage should be taken of all felicitous occasions and congress judiciously associated with the most happy times.

Especial care should be given to the preparatory

stage and deliberation exercised, with a view of producing the maximum ardor with its most profound reaction.

Each subsequent effort will prove less arduous, and persistent attempts will most often be rewarded by the most happy results.

Most rapid progress will be made by attention to the physical conditions, as the instinctive promptings naturally have a greater effect upon the disposition than the external influences.

Bodily changes always forcibly impress an ordinary mental state, for realities supplant fancy.

Genital hyperæmia is sure to awaken sexual thoughts, and desire is forthcoming with erectility.

By attention to the production of local distension, a desire for depletion is made imperative, and local measures should not be ignored or neglected.

Friction, massage, titillation or pressure become tantalizing manipulations, and those applications which produce temporary local turgidity, or swelling, produce sexual excitement, with its mental longing for pleasurable relief.

Greatly delayed sexual practices, or intercourse that has been postponed beyond the first half of woman's menstrual life, sometimes tends to establish a condition in which there is no response to the usual sexual stimulation.

The demands of sexual excitement may not be understood if they have not been met with until comparatively late in life, and women who have for years been trained to disregard their animal promptings often require powerful stimulation to awaken sexual emotion. Under ordinary circumstances such women would be left without any exalted feeling or marked circulatory change in their genitalia at the time of enforced cessation of copulative procedures. The active party will have developed in himself a state of excitement by his advances, and have persisted in his actions to the limit of his endurance, and still the woman is not moved to any excitement and does not respond to any available stimulation.

When the woman has been submitted with reasonable frequency to such stimulation as the husband can afford, and at such times when nature has made the starting point most propitious, and no impression is made upon her sexuality, the chances of developing desirable relations are very small and the case is practically hopeless unless outside aid is brought to bear.

Persuasion and argument are useless, for the mind cannot grasp what the senses are unaccustomed to, and the woman remains cold and unaffected during the embrace.

The only hope lies in rendering the sexual organs in such a state of functional activity as will command the mental concentration.

Upon the taking of bitters into the stomach, the gastric activity is stimulated and that organ prepared, by the secretion of its glands, for its work of digestion, and appetite for food is awakened which would not otherwise be felt.

By a similar stimulation of the genital organs, the glands become filled and the distention of the erectile tissues promotes secretion, which causes these organs to become in a state of preparation for the function for which they were designed, and thus sexual appetite is occasioned, which the mind cannot ignore and which would not otherwise take place.

A suggestion as to the significance of the peculiar sensation may be required, as the mind is not familiar with the feeling in its association with the sexual act, but nevertheless an alteration of general consciousness is caused in the same manner as the nutritive faculty is emphasized by the ingestion of a small amount of alcohol or a bitter substance into the stomach.

Cases of general debility or emaciation which are the result of worry or mental concentration are not at all rare and come under the physician's observation frequently.

There is, in thse cases, no derangement of the digestive organs themselves, but the mechanism is disturbed by the fixation of thought which, by its intensity, so absorbs the attention that the natural stimulus in the gastro-intestinal tract is not sufficient to make the impression required for a response, or reflex action, and hence there is no resultant activity of the organs, which means lack of motility.

This prevents the nutritive function from being active and there is no desire for food and the patient is with difficulty persuaded to take nourishment.

When the waste is not repaired, the energy required for animation is taken from the surplus material within the tissues, and weakness and emaciation result.

To overcome the condition it is necessary to re-establish the normal conditions for response, and this is done by either diverting the mind so that it will again be impressionable by the natural stimulation, or by increasing the intensity of the stimulus to such a degree as will make an impression upon the consciousness.

The most effective method of bringing about the condition in which the normal function is again aroused by natural means, is by both diminishing the mental concentration and employing extraordinary local stimulation to the digestive organs; and hence a change of scene or recreation is advised and an agent employed, or medicine given, which, by its presence, so acts upon the digestive tract as to produce increased circulation, or functional activity, and then the nutritive function again becomes active.

Coming down to the practical activity of the sexual function on the part of woman, it will be found that in married life as we find it to-day, the family consideration, or the concern about conception, is more or less constantly present and uppermost in the wifely mind.

This fixed thought or mental concentration is often very marked and forms the greatest impediment to natural relations, or the development of sexual equality.

So great is this concern in many instances that it amounts to actual and strong prejudice, which must be removed before natural inclinations will be yielded to. There is at times an unalterable determination to resist pregnancy, and dangerous practices are often resorted to for circumvention, regardless of the personal or family health and welfare.

Physicians are almost daily consulted about the best way out of the difficulty, and advice is demanded by the more intelligent and thoughtful.

The woman cannot properly fill her position as wife unless she is competent to supply what is necessary for the satisfaction of the sexual function.

By giving that which gratifies the dictates of the normal manhood of to-day, she will discharge her womanly obligation and bring upon herself a condition that is healthful and, therefore, attractive, together with such a mental state as will make her disposition admirable and amiable.

First of all she should remember her humanity and judiciously keep in control, but not persistently suppress, her sexual prompting.

Willingness may be shown by silent acquiescence, and active response, as excitement increases, is indicated.

By gentle, playful resistance and half-concealed attractions, the imagination is exercised and mutual desire originated, but a combative attitude and lack of active co-operation when excitation has been established should not be exhibited.

Hasty action on the part of the aggressor may be discouraged, but personal desire should be warmly welcomed.

There should be no submission in the absence of emotion, but the greater the display of animation after union, the more effective and complete the coupling.

Elimination of fear is essential, and there should be no progressively suggestive actions permitted or excitement occasioned when natural intercourse is prohibited.

Solicitation is best conveyed by inference, but care should be taken that such be correctly interpreted. Whenever intercourse is attempted the climax should at all times be diligently sought, and personal methods to effect its timely occurrence should be practiced.

Some way of expressing the satisfaction derived will be helpful, though it is not necessary that this should be voluntarily voiced, but any derogatory remarks had best be discreetly avoided.

By the use of a little tact and intelligent consideration, any ordinary young wife would, by governing her conduct in accordance with the foregoing, do her part in developing a sexual equality that could scarcely be disappointing and which would render her sexual relations very much as she made them, and to her own liking.

Evolution that brings about peace and happiness is always to be commended, and revolution in domestic relations, as elsewhere, is to be discouraged, for it rarely, if ever, does any good.

It may be said by some that we have, in these pages, unnecessarily gone into detail about a delicate and unspeakable matter, but attention to detail is the secret of success in the practice of medicine, or any other venture, and great calamities often occur because little things have been neglected.

More suffering is caused by ignorance of these matters than by all other causes. If we made as great a mystery of our digestive function as we do about our sexual function, and never dared to speak about eating or preparing food; wrote novels filled with descriptions of the pleasures and pains of pursuing uncooked food, but never dared to refer to the ultimate intention of our heroes to eat that food; and if the novelist who did dare to speak of that intention in a most indirectly suggestive way, was branded as an infamous writer of immoral books—the misery of mankind would be transferred from the sexual apparatus to the digestive.

What now passes for sexual physiology is, as a matter of fact, in reality, sexual theology. It still remains true that most people who are seriously distressed on account of their sexual functions are not the victims of any disease, and do not require anything for their relief besides a little scientific knowledge, and information and advice that is practical.

The cause and effect having been pointed out, with the condition amenable to control, the treatment and relief should be comparatively simple and easy.

CHAPTER X

COPULATION AND PROPAGATION.

Nature Satisfied only with Expression of Love—Desire for Coupling most Persistent—Congress for Purpose of Procreation only is Impractical—Self-Control—Emotion Never Aroused by Thoughts of Offspring—The Testicles and Their Product—Semen Expelled with Evacuations—Conditions with Premature Emission—Development of Sex Glands—Menstruation and Ovulation—Upon what Menstruation Depends—When Graafian Follicles Rupture—Jewish Law Prohibits Congress for Seven Days after Flow—Hebrew Customs—Average Duration of Pregnancy 278 Days—Rules for Time of Delivery—Properties of Ova and Spermatozoa—When their Vitality is Lost and how Affected—Differences in Procreative Ability—Plural Births and Possibilities of Conception—The Sexual Act and Ovulation—Only Way of Calculating Gestation—Laws upon Legitimacy—Site of Impregnation—Ovum Fertilized Two or Three Days After Rupture Only—Duration of Menses makes Time of Pregnancy Vary—Woman's Feelings a Guide to Exact Time of Ovulation—The Popular Belief and the Periods when Intercourse is most Effectual for Pregnancy—Intelligent Government of Sexual Habits—Influence upon Progeny—Pre-determination of Sex—Maternal Impressions—In Education Lies only Hope of Preventing Derogatory Acts.

The best thing and the great thing in life is health, which means happiness and holiness.

The best kind of happiness is the happiness of being alive, and the best expression of animation is an activity in rythm with the universe.

It is ignorance, pure and simple, to say that an ordinary man or woman can be in harmony with fellow beings on this mundane sphere and not be actuated by what enlivens everything else that lives.

Nothing will satisfy nature but an expression of love, and if we are contented, as nature intended we should be, we will possess the ability to receive and bestow the manifestations of life in a manner that is human.

A man would have to be a saint and a woman an angel if they were to live together on this planet and never consider their relations from a physical standpoint.

Acts of a sexual nature are prevented only by restricted freedom or inability, and the possibility of ignoring the physical contact between the sexes exists only in the minds of the erratic and fanciful.

Platonic affection is a good subject to teach, but it is not strictly practiced without difficulty, and such a friendship will, in nearly all instances, be exclusively lived only by those who are too young to understand or those who have lived the allotted time of man and have passed beyond the possibility of natural delight.

The desire for coupling is the most persistent, familiar and fascinating feeling that engages and actuates both men and women.

Because of the masterful creative impulse throughout the entire universe, evidences which call to mind the underlying plan are on every hand and the temptations encountered are numerous and powerful.

Only those who are half-born, immature or partly dead are free from this influence, for a susceptibility betokens a fullness of life and a reservoir of love for the living.

The theory tnat congress should be had only for the purpose of procreation will always remain a theory by reason of its absurdity.

So long as human beings have organs whose functions cannot be ignored and whose activity creates emotion, so long will the being clamor to put these organs to use in the manner designed by creation.

Whenever normal men and women are free to act, and understand themselves and each other, they will be drawn together, and the closeness of their union will depend only upon their feeling of liberty.

It was ever thus and will always remain so—unless they are reconstructed and cast in a different mould—any teaching or opinion to the contrary notwithstanding.

Any doctrine tending to the elimination of gender will find adherents only among those who are themselves already neutral.

Self-control is admirable and indicative of strength of character. It should be commended and practiced always, but only up to the point of retaining the highest manhood or womanhood.

No good can ever come to a people when they completely resign their individuality and never assert their inherent rights.

While men continue to possess organs that will elaborate and discharge the vital fluid, and until women cease to demonstrate by their menstruation that they have reproductive organs and are fruitful, there will be sexual congress.

The idea that the millenium would be reached when there would be no more sexual intercourse could only prevail in a being that was but half alive.

It would be necessary in order to bring about this state, to deprive the male of his masculine organs by castration, and, curiously enough, this method has been advocated.

The plan, as outlined by a visionary female, is to have the testicles of all male infants removed, with the exception of one in every community, who should be used for breeding purposes.

He should be the finest specimen of manhood to be found and everything to make him as nearly perfect physically as is possible should be done.

For the satisfaction of the maternal instinct, those women who were desirous of becoming mothers would be permitted to go and have some of the semen, which could be artificially taken from this one and only man, inserted into their bodies without any physical contact with its producer.

The idea was to improve the race, and the female physician in Boston who advocated the adoption of such a plan had in view the relief of woman from the "humiliation" of submitting to sexual intercourse, as well as the prevention of assaults upon females.

There is, of course, not the slightest chance of this method ever being attempted, as neither women nor men who are normal desire relief of that kind and could not under any consideration even be brought to entertain such a notion.

No sane men can be found who will voluntarily part with their testicles, and high-minded women very much prefer to know and be with the father of their children to the exclusion of all others.

Sexual congress is possible only with sexual excitement, and the thought of offspring alone would never arouse the emotions and bring about this condition.

When nature does not unconsciously establish the state it is normally brought about by association, in fact or in thought, with a desirable member of the opposite sex.

In the course of nature children are born, but they come as the result of created circumstances, and in that manner only.

The essential elements for propagation are continuously being formed in healthy adults, and when favorable conditions for growth are not secured these are discharged, and the process of elaboration is continued.

The male organs which produce the essential element are the testicles, from whence come the spermatozoa.

The spermatozoa are derived from the cells of the two globular bodies which are suspended within the scrotum, and their occurrence in the impregnating fluid of nearly all kinds of animals proves that they are essential to fecundation, and their actual contact with the ovum of the female is necessary for its development into a fœtus.

The spermatozoa are composed of heads with comparatively long tails, and are possessed of the power of motion to an unusual degree. Gibbes concluded that the motive power lies, in a great measure, in the filament and the membrane which attaches it to the body.

When alive this filament is in constant motion, which is at first so quick that it is difficult to see, but as its vitality becomes impaired the motion becomes slower, and is then easily perceived to be a continuous waving from side to side.

After puberty there is a constant secretion of seminal fluid in the tubules of the testicles.

Ordinarily the fluid is secreted very slowly, but under excitement the quantity is greatly increased.

By means of the convoluted vasa deferentia, the secretion is passed into the seminal vesicles at the base of the bladder.

These vesicles serve as reservoirs for the fluid and also secrete a liquid that is added to the secretion of the testicles and which seems necessary for the proper composition of the semen.

In some of the lower animals these vesicles do not communicate with the vasa deferentia, but discharge their contents directly into the urethra.

In all animals in whom they are found, and in whom the sexual function is exercised at only one season of the year, the seminal vesicles, as well as the testicles, become enlarged at the approach of that period.

The secretions of the prostate and Cowper's glands are also added to the seminal fluid, but their nature and purpose have not been definitely determined.

When the seminal fluid is not expelled during an

emission by orgasm, it may be discharged slowly and in small quantities into the urethra and expelled with the evacuations.

Under the stimulus of excitement, when there is congestion of the sexual organs, a much larger quantity of the fluid is elaborated and secreted.

Sometimes, after dallying with women, and when no connection is had, men experience a fullness or aching in the testicles, and not infrequently after such a time the ejaculation center is excited to reflex action, and emission occurs during sleep.

Very often, especially in the younger men, or those not accustomed to intercourse with the party, there will be a reflex or premature emission, owing to the fullness of the seminal tract and the inability of the mind to control the lower center.

The untimely and disappointing discharge may occur before a vigorous erection has been established and the fluid emitted is probably largely composed of the prostatic and vesicle secretions, with comparatively few spermatozoa.

In such cases it is usually more thin and watery in appearance than that which comes from the deeper seminal tract.

Under such conditions the ardor will be diminished and the sensations experienced less pronounced than with a definite and full orgasm, such as usually occurs when copulation has been entirely successful and complete.

Sensitiveness or irritability of the posterior urethra, as well as the inflammation of gonorrhœa, causes the same state of affairs to be brought about.

When there is no lesion in the genito-urinary tract no alarm need be felt, as the ability to retain the emission a given time and the ardor accompanying the orgasm varies in the same individual as well as in different men.

As familiarity with the habit is acquired and the acts repeated without too great length of intermission, the disappointment will be overcome and the emission deposited where it naturally should be, and at the proper time.

The generative glands are developed from the same fœtal structure, the Wolffian bodies, and what becomes the testicle of the male grows to form the ovary in the female.

In the ovary is formed the female element, or egg, which must necessarily come in contact with the germ derived from the testicle before fecundation can occur.

Whether sexual union takes place or not, the ova are developed and discharged, and the process of ovulation occurs in connection with the female's menstruation.

The exact relation between the menstrual discharge and ovulation is not altogether clear, nor is the primary cause of the menstrual flow established with entire satisfaction.

What is known as heat, or rut, in the lower animals, and menstruation in the human female, are practically the same phenomena, for though there may be some minor differences of detail, yet the periods correspond.

In animals who are capable of impregnation at

regular periods, as in the human subject, the ova appear at maturity and are always discharged at such times. It is only at such a time when a mature ovum has ruptured from the ovary that impregnation can occur.

The separation of the matured ovum, or egg, from the ovary occurs periodically at or about the epochs of menstruation, although not always with exact coincidence.

Rupture of Graafian follicle, which contains the ovum, does not happen on the same day of the monthly period in all women.

Whether this always occurs just before, during or immediately after the flow is not demonstrable.

Upon examination of either of the two ovaries, which each female possesses, it will be found that there are a number of Graafian follicles in different stages of development and also evidences of one or more follicles having been ruptured.

Menstruation is a periodical bloody discharge from the womb which occurs in the healthy woman about every 28 days, from the time of puberty to the change of life. This process is, as a rule, suspended during pregnancy and the time of nursing.

The duration of the period and the amount of discharge varies considerably in different women within normal limits, and also in the same woman at different times.

In this country the average duration is probably about four days, or from three to six, though it may habitually be even less, or more, and still not be abnormal.

The amount of fluid discharged is given at from two to six ounces, but this, too, is subject to great variations among healthy women.

The flow comes from the interior of the womb and, when discharged, consists of blood, mucus and remnants of the epithelial lining of the uterus.

Whether menstruation is the result of congestion alone, or is a destructive process by which the preparation for an impregnation is carried away, has been the subject for considerable discussion.

Kirke believes it to be "not the sign of the capability of being impregnated as much as of disappointed impregnation."

The process depends, wholly or in part, upon the escape of one or more ovules from the ovary; upon congestion or vascular engorgement of the generative organs, and the transudation of blood from the vessels supplying the interior of the womb.

It has been held that the flow was the result of uterine congestion arising from the enlargement of a Graafian follicle and the escape of an ovule from the ovary, but though this occurs, as a rule, at each menstrual period, yet it may occur in the absence of menstruation.

Cases of impregnation have occurred in women during the period of lactation, and in amenorrhœa, when the monthly flow is absent.

In animals connection never takes place except during the rut, and it is then only that the female is capable of conception, but in the human being conception occurs in the intervals between the periods.

This argument has been brought against the

theory that ovulation is the cause of menstruation, for it is said that if menstruation depends upon the rupture of a Graafian follicle and the liberation of an ovule, then impregnation could only take place during or immediately after menstruation.

Coste endeavors to explain this by supposing that it is the maturing of the Graafian follicle that occasions menstruation and not its rupture, and that the follicle may remain unruptured for a considerable time after it is mature, and its subsequent liberation be determined by some other cause, such as sexual excitement.

In a woman who died on the first day of mestruation Coste found a recently ruptured follicle; in another instance, at a more advanced period and toward the decline of the menstrual flow, he found evidences that the rupture had occurred later; in the case of a female who drowned herself four or five days after the cessation of the menses, a follicle was found in the right ovary, so distended that it was ruptured by very slight pressure; and other instances were observed in which follicles were not ruptured during the menstrual period.

Doubtless nature intended that menstruation should not be accompanied by any special pain or discomfort, but unfortunately the function is by no means so regular, normal or physiological in a great many women of our day.

The high tension put upon the constitution by the requirements of civilization, the social and home cares, the mental and physical strain to which women are subjected, together with various habits of life which conflict with natural living, are some of the causes which have contributed to place woman in a position where menstruation is very often painful, and have led to the habit of alluding to the period as the time of her sickness.

There is a prevailing opinion that conception is most likely to follow an intercourse which occurs soon after a monthly period, but it is certain that it does occur at other times, and may take place at a time far removed from menstruation.

It is probable that there is presented a favorable condition for the occurrence of fecundation in the fact that there is unusual sexual excitement generally experienced by many females immediately after menstruation has ceased; and this added to the condition of the female generative organs during this period of the month, and their action during and after coitus, usually makes this time the most favorable for impregnation.

For the Jewish people there is a law which prohibits sexual intercourse for seven days after the cessation of menstruation.

This law is almost universally observed by these women and even those who observe no other ceremonial law, cling to it after everything else is ignored.

When the flow lasts only for a few hours, the five days during which the period might continue are observed, and to this is added the seven clear days, making twelve days per period in which connection is not allowed.

Should any discharge be seen in the inter-menstrual period, seven days would have to be kept, but not the five, for such irregular, unusual discharge.

The "bath of purification" is used on the last night of the seven clear days. (Playfair)

The custom of the Jews, who are a prolific race, indicates that conception occurs with contact before the menstrual flow, and this, together with the anatomical condition of the womb just before the period, seems to show that the ovum fertilized is the one which is discharged in connection with the expected flow and not with the previous menstruation.

Most married women make some effort to keep track of their menstrual periods, and it may be assumed that the Jewish people, knowing as they do that they will be deprived of intercourse for at least twelve days, would be especially careful in marking these epochs.

In this connection it may be recalled that it is but human for them to be very solicitous, and their large number of children could be readily accounted for by supposing that they would naturally cohabit, with a degree of regularity, as close to the expected appearance of the flow as was convenient and practical.

It is very probable that conception occurs nearly always in the Fallopian tube, and most often in its outer portion.

Cases of extra uterine pregnancy occur in rare instances, in which the ovule has become impregnated but has failed to enter the tube.

The precise duration of pregnancy in a given case (reckoning from the time of intercourse) is unreliable, as it is very probable that in the human female, as in the lower animals, a considerable but unknown interval may occur between insemination and impregnation.

The time of the delivery of the child is usually determined by the date of the cessation of the last menstruation, and the average for this time is 278 days.

Nægeli's method was to count seven days from the first appearance of the last menstruation and then subtract three months from the year. Thus, if a woman began to menstruate on August 10, by adding seven days we have the date of August 17, and subtracting three months would give May 17 as the probable date of delivery.

Mathews Duncan has made a careful study of the period of gestation and uses the following rule:

"Find the day on which the female ceased to menstruate, or the first day of being what she calls 'well'. Take that day nine months forward as 275—unless February is included, in which case it is taken as 273—days. To this add three days in the former case or five if February is in the count, to make up the 278. This 278th day should then be fixed as the middle of the week, or to make the prediction the more accurate, of the fortnight, in which the confinement is likely to occur. By this means allowance is made for the average variation of either excess or deficiency."

To obtain a clear understanding of when conception actually occurs it will be necessary to consider both the passage of the ovule in its course through the female genital tract, and also the properties of the spermatozoa in the semen that has been deposited.

Sexual excitement and orgasm in the female with

the necessary congestion, no doubt influences and favors the rupture of the Graafian follicle and enhances ovulation, though this process occurs whether desire and pleasure are felt or not.

Kisch states that an unfaithful wife is more likely to conceive with her lover than with her husband, and believes that in a majority of women sexual pleasure only appears gradually, after the first cohabitation, and then develops progressively, and that the first conception often coincides with its complete awakening. In 556 cases of his own, the most frequent epoch of first impregnation was found to be between ten and fifteen months after marriage.

In some childless women impregnation has been successful after the production of pleasurable coitus.

The time required for the passage of the ovum through the Fallopian tube to the womb may be from eight to ten days.

During its passage it accumulates and becomes invested with a covering of albuminous material which is deposited around it in successive layers, the thickness of which varies in different animals.

This covering is very abundant in birds, in which it forms the familiar white of the egg.

Coste believes that this albuminous covering is impermeable to the spermatozoa and this, together with the rapid degenerative changes in the ovum itself, prevents its impregnation.

He concludes, therefore, that conception can occur only very near the ovary, or just about the fimbriated extremity of the Fallopian tube.

Nearly all authorities agree that conception does

not take place after the ovum has reached the uterus, but in an effort to explain those cases in which pregnancy is supposed to have gone beyond the natural limit of 280 days from the cessation of the menses, Lœwenthal has proposed the hypothesis that the ovum reaches the uterine cavity unimpregnated—that if impregnated at this time menstruation does not occur, and the ovum settles itself in the new-formed mucus membrane prepared for the next menstrual period. If, however, impregnation does not take place, the ovum perishes, and its death causes an active congestion which is followed by menstruation.

Such cases may be explained, however, by the fact that ovulation, which makes conception possible, may occur between the periods of uterine hemorrhage.

The spermatozoa of the male testicles have been found alive and in motion throughout the entire generative tract of the female.

They have many times been found on the surface of the ovaries some days after coitus.

Their movements are said to continue from twenty-four to forty-eight hours outside of the body, but they are active in the uterus and Fallopian tubes for six or seven days after emission.

The experiments of Haussman show that the spermatozoa lose their power of motion in the vagina within twelve hours after coitus, and hence cannot be fructifying.

The male element necessary for fecundation finds its way into the Fallopian tube of the female very largely by reason of its own inherent motive power.

These spermatozoa, which are found in large numbers in the seminal fluid, thrive in the alkaline mucus of the internal female organs, which actually favors their movement.

They are not arrested by contact with the menstrual blood.

Water speedily arrests these movements which may be restored by the addition of dense saline and other solutions.

All of the alkaline animal fluids of moderate viscidity favor the movements, while the action of acid or of very dilute solutions is unfavorable.

The movements are suspended by extreme cold, but they return when the ordinary temperature is restored. (Flint.)

So much vitality do these spermatozoa possess and so great is their motility that cases have been known in which pregnancy has occurred without actual sexual connection, but where the semen has been deposited at the vaginal orifice.

Authenticated cases have been cited where the hymen has remained intact and prevented the introduction of the male organ into the vagina and still pregnancy has resulted.

In such an event it is necessary that the spermatozoa, after being deposited on the mucus membrane near the entrance to the vagina, have made their way along the length of this canal, entered the cervix and passed upwards through the womb to, and possibly through, the Fallopian tube to meet with the ovule.

These cases, of course, are extremely rare, as such a procedure is little more than possible, and it is probable that, though the male organ did not actually gain complete entrance into the vagina, yet a portion of the semen had been ejaculated into the canal.

Breeders of valuable animals have taken advantage of the vitality of the male reproductive element and are continually putting this knowledge to good use.

Mares are not only fertilized by the seminal fluid from stallions without actual contact, but several are made to become with foal by the use of one emission, and the seminal fluid is even shipped to a distance for this purpose.

The procedure is conducted somewhat as follows: The stallion is permitted to cover one mare, and after intercourse, the major portion of the fluid ejaculated is, by means of a syringe or "impregnator," withdrawn from the vagina and a part thereof subsequently injected into another animal that has "come in," or is in the proper condition for impregnation.

The procedure is successfully carried out and good results obtained, and from four to eight mares are thus served by one standing, the writer has been informed by a veterinary surgeon.

There is quite a difference among women relative to their susceptiblity to conception.

Some women become pregnant with comparative readiness while others conceive with more difficulty. Men, too, possess a varying capacity for procreation.

This may be due to some weakness or deficiency, either hereditary or acquired, of the generative apparatus, or they may not naturally be the best of breeders.

It sometimes happens that during the first few

years of marriage the union will be fruitless, and that subsequently children appear with great regularity.

Occasionally it will be noticed that one marriage will be without issue, but when another is contracted it may prove fruitful.

In most cases it will be found that the state of health in one or the other, or perhaps both parties is, for the time being, below par, but there are so many things that may have a bearing upon the condition that no one definite cause can be assigned nor any rule formulated that would cover all cases.

That some few women may be liable to conception when intercourse is had at almost any time during the month must be admitted, and that plural births occur in every community is known by all.

Such unusual circumstances are not so difficult to understand and may be accounted for when the several established facts are considered.

Every normal female has two ovaries and in each of these may be found several Graafian follicles in different stages of development.

One of these follicles at least, is ruptured (and possibly more) with coincident congestion of the internal female organs.

Some women undoubtedly produce a larger number and more vigorous ova than others, as is found throughout all life.

The ovule remains in the tube a varying length of time, which may be eight or ten days; and the spermatozoa retain their vitality in the uterus for six or seven days, and perhaps longer.

This gives a period of seventeen days, or over

half the month, which may elapse between the time of ovulation and that of sexual connection, and in which there is a possibility of conception.

The probability of ovulation occurring in one or the other ovary under some unusual excitement or stimulation at an unusual time, or between the menstrual periods, explains (together with the seventeen days above given as the time limit for coalescence) the possibility of conception taking place at almost any time during the month.

It may be understood, however, that these are only possibilities, for it is not likely that such circumstances would be productive of a state of pregnancy, except in very rare instances, for even if the spermatozoa did come in contact with the ovule after either or both had been liberated sveral days, their vitality would have become impaired to such an extent as to make a healthy growth improbable.

The difficulty of determining the exact time of conception is made apparent by the variation of a week or ten days in the period of gestation, or the duration of fœtal life.

The average time given is 278 days, and Jewish women reckon their pregnancy to last nine calendar or ten lunar months—270 to 280 days. (Asher).

There is a point in this connection that, so far as I know, has not been considered in determining the exact time of the month when conception usually occurs.

There may be a difference in the time required for intra-uterine growth, or the period between the actual time of conception and the birth of the child.

If a number of hen's eggs be placed in an incubator and kept under the same conditions, it may be found that the chicks do not all make their appearance at exactly the same time. There will be a difference of some hours, or, it may be, a day or more, between the appearance of the first and last chick.

A difference of a day in the development of the embryonic chick, whose period of incubation is approximately twenty days, would, with the same ratio, make a difference of a dozen or more days in the gestation period of the human offspring.

If it were established that the actual time between conception and birth was different at different times—that is to say, that with the same time of conception there might be a difference of ten days in two given periods of gestation—it might serve as an aid in determining a more definite relation between ovulation and menstruation.

With the determination that ovulation occurs in most instances at a certain time with regard to menstruation, the time of conception could be given within smaller limits and the period when cohabitation would, or would not, lead to conception could be stated more definitely.

Nearly all authorities are agreed at the present time that conception occurs, in the vast majority of cases, in the outer portion of the Fallopian tube.

It is by no means certain that all, or even the majority of ova become fertilized by contact with spermatozoa or that all the fertilized ova become attached to the female womb, and thus find conditions favorable for development. The mucus membrane of the uterus must be in a condition to permit of the growth of the impregnated ovum or it perishes and is passed off.

It is supposed that after menstruation is the most favorable time for intra-uterine growth.

Other things being equal, the nearer the approach of the ovum to the uterine cavity, the less likely is conception to occur; and the longer the time that elapses between seminal ejaculation and the meeting of the spermatozoa with the ovum, the greater the improbability of conception.

In other words, the nearer the act of sexual intercourse is to the time of ovulation, the greater is the likelihood for resulting pregnancy.

The connection between ovulation and menstruation is fairly definite, and most conceptions take place about this time.

There certainly are exceptions, but they may not be very much more numerous than are plural births, and these are but of occasional occurrence.

If the conception did not occur in the great majority of cases at approximately the same time of the month relative to menstruation, the average duration of pregnancy would not be 278 days after the cessation of the flow.

The only way that pregnancy is ever calculated with any degree of reliability is by means of menstruation, and the cases in which pregnancy has resulted from one single coitus, the exact date of which is known with absolute certainty, are so few that sufficient data upon which to base a definite conclusion is not available. It would be asking too much of a reasonable number of perfectly reliable women to submit themselves to such exactions for the sole purpose and benefit of scietific investigation, and unless positive reliance can be had, the information is worthless.

In order to establish the legitimacy of children, some countries have enacted laws by which to establish the natural limits of pregnancy, and have designated the time beyond which it cannot continue.

The Roman law did not consider a child legitimate if born later than ten calendar months after its father's death.

The French law allows the legitimacy of a child born 300 days after the death or non-access of the husband.

The Prussian law declares a child legitimate that is born within 302 days after the husband's death.

In Scotland the legitimacy of a child is established if it is born within ten months after the death of the husband.

In this country and in England there are no laws regulating the exact period of gestation in relation to legitimacy, each case being decided on its own merits. (Reese)

Without regard to the time of copulation, the overwhelming majority of births would indicate that the duration of gestation varies but a few days, and hence it seems a fair conclusion to assume that conception occurs in most instances at practically the same time of the month.

This time of conception, it would be rational to maintain, is during the first two or three days immediately after the liberation of the ovule from the ovary.

The difference in the duration of the menstrual epoch is often from two to four days, for some women menstruate only two or three days and others continue to flow six, or even more.

These few days of variation in time added to the menstrual period would make it appear that pregnancy was three days shorter in the cases of prolonged menstruation, when in reality it was the same length of time, as the date of the beginning of the term was fixed by the cessation of the flow.

The largest percentage of deliveries occurs between the 274th and 280th day after the flow. (Playfair.)

This is the time given in ordinary women, but it will be noticed that the Jews, who do not copulate for a week after menstruation, give a wider latitude —making it 270 to 280—thus allowing for the difference in the number of days that women commonly menstruate.

The popular belief that conception occurs more readily and most frequently when intercourse is had during the first few days after the menses, is not without foundation.

At the beginning of menstruation the mucus membrane of the womb is congested and swollen, and more or less completely fills in the uterine cavity, this would tend to prevent the free ascent of the spermatazoa and also be an unfavorable condition for the ovule to become fixed in the cavity, as the shedding of the membrane would disturb its fixation;

while the anatomical condition of the womb after the old membrane is cast off and the new one is being formed is a more favorable time for the beginning of pregnancy.

Though the ascent of the spermatozoa may be more difficult with the swollen condition of the intra-uterine mucus membrane, yet in the case of the Jewish women there would be little liability to disturbance of uterine tranquility by the passionate orgasm of coitus during the week when the womb is in the best condition to receive the impregnated ovum.

Agitation or uterine activity may at any time cause a blighting of the ovum, and these women are not subjected to the rythmical movements of the womb at the most critical time, or when the ovum may be most easily dislodged.

This disturbance of uterine tranquility may serve to explain also why women who are very passionate and have a pronounced orgasm, do not, as a rule, (by reason of the repeated agitation of the womb incident to coitus at this most critical time) conceive as readily as others who are more listless; for it has been noticed that those who are exceptionally passionate and indulge in frequent, violent intercourse at this time of the month oftentimes do not reach pregnancy.

Some women are said to experience certain peculiar sensations some hours after coitus, which are supposed to indicate that conception has taken place, but these are not at all reliable as conception is usually as insensible as digestion.

To summarize, it may reasonably be stated that conception, in the average case, is usually limited to those two or three days in the menstrual month which immediately follow the actual separation of the ovule from the ovary.

Pregnancy is likely to result from sexual connection during the time, or within two or three days thereof, though with the greatest likelihood during the recent freedom of the ovule.

Allowing three days for variation in the time of ovulation, and taking the time before, during and after this event, we have a period of nine days, or about one-third of the month in which copulation may prove fruitful.

This may be taken as the usual time when pregnancy is begun, but it must be understood that it is by no means always limited to this time.

Undoubtedly the overwhelming majority of cases in which pregnancy occurs is confined to these limits, and the exceptions are so few that the percentage could probably be counted upon the fingers of one hand.

Some women experience the greatest intensity of sexual feeling before their menstrual periods, while others are conscious of more pronounced emotion after menstruation. In this circumstance may be found a guide as to the probable relation of menstruation with ovulation in a given case.

The emotion might not unreasonably be attributed to the liberation of the ovule, and if a woman habitually felt the strongest sexual inclination before the flow, it could be inferred that ovulation in her case occurred near the beginning of her menses; whereas, if she were in the habit of becoming more passionate after the flow had ceased, she might assume that with her the ovule was set free at the termination of her period.

Copulation soon after the flow has ceased is probably the most effectual for pregnancy, though just before the period is also a very propitious time.

Given the assurance of the exact time of ovulation, a woman's sexual habits could then be intelligently governed accordingly.

Just what it is that makes the seminal fluid capable of impregnating the ovum and of transmitting to the developing offspring the character of the father has not been determined.

It is known that the physical characteristics, such as color, features, size, mental disposition and liability to disease are imparted to the child, and not only that, but subsequent children may be influenced by previous conceptions and partake of the nature of a grandparent or one by whom the woman has previously borne a child.

In animals a previous pregnancy may have an influence upon the progeny, and a woman may, by a second husband, have children who resemble somewhat her previous husband, but the fact remains unexplained and no cause for this strange and remarkable circumstance can be given.

The pre-determination of sex has been a favorite topic for speculative theorizing, but no plausible theory has yet been advanced that proves applicable to a majority of cases, and the sexes of the children that are born continue to be in about equal proportion.

Some families contain a much larger number of girls than boys, and vice versa, but no one has yet formulated a plan whereby the sexes can be effectively regulated, and so this, too, must be classed among the impenetrable mysteries.

The question whether impressions made upon the nervous system of the mother can exert an influence upon the unborn child, has always been an interesting one.

"Like begets like" throughout nature, and while most authors admit that violent emotions experienced by the mother may effect the nutrition and general development of the fœtus, many authorities of note deny that the imagination can have any influence in producing deformities, or physical abnormalities.

The power of mind is tremendous, and thoughts exert very great influence.

Sometimes the progeny assumes more the character of the male than the female parent, and sometimes the reverse is the case, without reference to the sex of the child. The habits of thought and disposition of the mother during her pregnancy may, to a considerable degree, influence the temperament and inclination of the child, and she could be especially careful of her habits and conduct during this period.

Those remarkable cases recorded as instances of marked children due to the influences of the maternal mind are not altogether reliable, for it most often happens that when a child is born with a deformity the mother imagines and seeks to explain it by some impression received during pregnancy, which she only recalls after the condition becomes apparent.

There is no satisfactory proof that the maternal mind has anything to do with the production of physical deformities during the pre-natal period.

Life manifests itself by birth, growth, development, decline and death. The germ of the being may be defined as that portion of the parent which is set apart with power to grow up into the likeness of the being from which it is derived.

In the least developed forms of life, almost any part of the body is capable of assuming the characters of a separate individual; in beings a little higher in rank, only a special part of the body can become a separate being, and only by conjugation with another special part; and in all animals but the lowest, and in some plants, the portions of organized structure specialized for development after their mutual union into a new individual, are formed on two distinct beings, which we call respectively the male and female.

The ordinary life is liberally punctuated with the causes that lead to sexual excitement, and a better knowledge and understanding of the relations between copulation and propagation will ever tend to the uplifting of humanity and prevent acts which must needs be derogatory to health and happiness.

Sexual practices of some sort will continue so long as there is a susceptibility to excitement, and in education lies the only hope of bringing about more amicable relations between husband and wife.

CHAPTER XI

NERVOUS WOMEN.

Nervous Condition one in which the Person is Unduly Excited and Deficient in Control—Exhaustion of Nerve Force and Debility of Centers—Abnormal Response the Essential Feature—Neurasthenia Inherited and Acquired—Lack of Endurance and Failure of Mutual Support—Reserve Power and Neurotic Tendency—Irritable Weakness—First Manifestation is Worry—Weakest Function Early Involved—Love, Religion and the Sexual Passion as the Causes in the Female—Signs of Nervous Weakness in Young Women—Nervousness Relieved by Marriage—Sense of Fatigue may be Purely Mental—Numerous Fears—Loss of Power in Fixed Attention—Spinal Symptoms—Circulatory Changes—Frequent Disorders of Sight—Morbid Action of Vaso-Motor System—Greatest Number of Dyspepsias are Nervous—Disturbance of Sexual Organs most Frequent of all in Neurasthenia—Surgery in Pelvic Disorders and its Most Powerful Factor—Nervous Weakness as Primary Cause in Cases of Faulty Metabolism—Fat and Anæmic Type of Neurotic Persons—The Intellectual Type—Difference between Hysterical and Neurotic Women—Relation of Nervousness to Organic Disease—Nature Evolves but Does not Destroy Nor Save—Most Exacting Epochs in Woman's Career—Marriage Excites Sex Function—Circumstances Affect Women as Climate does Vegetation—Monotony is Unfavorable—Reflex Actions—How Nervousness is Acquired—Neurosis Occur Chiefly with Generative Disorders—Physiological Means of Relief—Medicine as a Spur to Nature—Treatment of Depression—The Great Cause of Domestic Infelicity—How Harmony is Restored—Conclusions.

When there is a state of steadiness, force of self-command, the person is said to possess good nerve; but where there is a condition of hyperæsthesia which makes the individual easily agitated, unusually susceptible or readily irritated and lacking in control, we are in the habit of calling such a person "nervous."

Nervousness, or neurasthenia, means without nerve strength, and is a deficiency or exhaustion of nervous force, as well as debility of the nervous centers.

The term neurasthenia is used to cover a group of symptoms which may be either general, and the expression of a derangement of the entire system; or local, and limited to certain organs. Thus we have gastric, cerebral, spinal, cardiac and sexual neurasthenia.

The essential feature in the condition is an abnormal response to stimuli, either from within or without, upon the higher centers which control the mind and preside over the functions of organic life.

There are certain mental states from which neurasthenia can with difficulty be differentiated at all times, and no definite line can always be drawn between this ailment and hysteria, hypochondriasis or insanity, as the one merges into the other.

Neurasthenia is generally designated as being hereditary or acquired, and it has come to indicate certain states of the nervous system for which the anatomatical basis is not clearly shown; but which are characterized by a lack of vigor, efficiency and endurance that usually effect a large number of nervous functions; and also by signs of active derangement which appear as positive symptoms, or are due to a failure of the mental support and control which the different parts of the nervous system give to each other in a state of health.

We do not all begin life with the same amount of nerve capacity, for parents who have been subject to nervous complaints or mental troubles transmit to their children an organization that is deficient in what may be called "nerve force."

So long as individuals with a neurotic tendency live under conditions that do not require the expenditure of more than moderate energy, no harm comes to them, but they are possessed of no reserve force, and in the emergencies to which every life is exposed, and which arise constantly in modern society, but become more exacting at certain times, these poorly equipped persons suffer under the strain and become bankrupt.

The functions of the body may also be disturbed and damaged by exercise or excitement which is excessive in proportion to the strength.

Those persons who start handicapped are most readily affected and their functions perverted, but a great deal of the nervousness of to-day is acquired. Many people begin life with a good supply of inherited energy and strength, but the many exigencies demand an unequal expenditure, and when a little additional force is required to be exerted in one direction it becomes a strain upon the organism and is not borne without distress.

Any ordinary excitement or exertion which is prolonged and, it may be, only slightly exaggerated, becomes excessive and wearing, and is most often first manifested as worry.

The person loses the faculty of distinction between the essentials and non-essentials, little things cause annoyance and those trifles which are ordinarily met with indifference become irritating, and then the entire organism reacts with undue readiness to slight stimuli.

The balance is with difficulty maintained and gradually the individual passes into a condition of irritable weakness.

When the equilibrium is restored by a relief of the tension by physiological processes or a removal of the exciting causes, the susceptibility to embarrassment is diminished and the person again becomes able to withstand the ordinary requirements of society.

In this country a very large proportion of nervousness is due to excessive waste of energy or vitality without recuperative power of the system as a whole, and the condition becomes manifested in the weakest organ or function of the body.

Among men, the business cares constantly increase the number of neurasthenics, but other very potent and frequent causes are the anxieties attendant upon love affairs, religious matters, and the sexual passion, which more particularly affect our women.

What is called hysteria in women is in many ways like what is termed neurasthenia in men, and by reason of its being in them the equivalent, neurasthenia is said to be almost as common among men as among women, but relatively there are very many more "nervous" women than there are men.

Neurasthenia in its full development is essentially a disease of puberty and middle life, though signs of a tendency in this direction are to be found in early life and consist in a general mobility of temperament, oversensitiveness or precociousness, and the occurrence of such symptoms as night terror, chorea, sleeplessness, etc.

In young women from sixteen to twenty years of age, various other signs of nervous weakness make their appearance, such as headache, backache, extreme and causeless lassitude. These years constitute in fact a critical period during which many are nervous invalids who may later again acquire good health.

Very often these periods of prostration are attributed to special causes, such as falls, overexertion, and the like, but these events are rarely more than exciting causes, and are not necessary to the result.

Such attacks are often diagnosticated as anæmia, or chlorosis, or as "spinal concussion," but their failure to respond to ordinary tonic or local treatment, and the fact that they are often relieved by means addressed to the general nervous condition, point to their true origin. Of course, true anæmia may complicate this condition of nervous prostration, or even act as its cause, and may require its own special treatment; but the important point is that the nervous element in the case is not to be overlooked. (Putnam.)

Neurasthenia is not likely to shorten life to any marked degree, unless it causes severe disorders of the nutrition. It does, however, occasionally happen that a patient dies from no other apparent cause than a prostration of the nervous functions.

Strictly speaking, neurasthenia is an inherited weakness of the nervous system, and in this sense is not curable.

It is, however, often possible to remove the patient from the circumstances which call out the manifestations of this weakness and thus practically effect a cure. Sometimes even with the best of treatment partial improvement and frequent relapses are the rule.

Constant watchfulness and good judgment rarely fail to bring some amelioration.

Acquired neurasthenia may pass away with the cessation of its cause, or may overlast this for many years, as in some cases of railway accidents, or similar injuries, and in the case of neurasthenia of the menopause. (Waterman and Putnam.)

Though the symptoms of this neurasthenic condition are extremely varied, and may be either general or localized; yet in most instances there will be a combination of both.

We have to recognize and not lose sight of the fact that there is a background of general nervous weakness, and that some one symptom may be so prominent that it seems to stand almost alone.

Some cases present almost exclusively mental symptoms and cannot bear a slight emotional strain without great suffering, though they show ordinary physical strength and endurance; while with others the muscular system is chiefly affected, and a great many manifest by far the most prominent symptoms in connection with the generative function.

The term "irritable weakness" expresses and indicates the character of most of the conditions that are met with.

A sense of fatigue is usually one of the chief symptoms in a neurasthenic individual, and it is possible that the tired feeling may be due to actual pathological changes in the nervous system.

Hodge has shown that fatigue in animals is accompanied by degenerative changes in the protoplasm and nuclei of their ganglion cells, and this may be an underlying cause in some instances; but, on the other hand, the weariness is very apt to be a purely psychological symptom, or the result of inharmonious brain action in which the several parts may be wholly normal.

Persons with a neurotic temperament are mostly quick, sensitive and versatile; are very often talented and intellectual, though rarely robust and capable of endurance.

They are frequently self-conscious and distrustful of themselves, and eventually become suspicious toward others and acquire a feeling of dread and isolation.

Some can hardly persuade themselves into a positive decision or exertion, but when under the influence of some slight excitement they may act with energy and intelligence.

Besides a mental instability, some patients who seem to have good control and are apparently well balanced, become, with provoking and unexplainable readiness, susceptible to trifling causes that may excite and maintain dyspepsia, loss of sleep, neuralgic disturbances and even collapse of strength. They often have numerous fears and dread to do things that ordinarily are undertaken without misgivings.

When the cerebral symptoms are more prominent, there may be inability to perform ordinary mental work.

The transactions of the details of business require

an effort, and there is loss in the power of fixation or attention.

A few may be cheerful and good tempered, but the majority are fretful, moody, irritable and depressed.

With more pronounced spinal symptoms may be found weariness with little physical exertion, pain in the back and aching of the legs, with increased reflexes and a feeling of numbness and tingling.

There is often a distressing sense of pressure at the top or back of the head, which is accompanied with tenderness and stiffness of the muscles at the back of the neck.

Palpitation of the heart and a beating or throbbing of the aorta in the region of the stomach is often annoying to these patients, and a nervous cough, which may be marked and obstinate, but without any local cause, is sometimes harrassing for an indefinite period.

The most important and frequent disturbances of the special senses are disorders of sight. This is often quite severe, and some patients who may have otherwise no more serious trouble than a certain delicacy of health, are for a long time quite unable to use their eyes for much reading or any fine work. This inability may be due in part, or wholly, to weakness of the power of accommodation and is often relieved by a systematic method of exercise, combined with the adjustment of suitable glasses.

Among the other morbid feelings with which neurasthenics are liable to be attacked are "hot flashes," which are often a serious annoyance and sometimes attended with visible flushing of the face and hands, and sensations of fullness and pulsation in the head.

Nervous persons are prone to blush easily, which fact usually indicates only a general emotional excitability, but they often show symptoms which may fairly be attributed to a morbid action of the vaso-motor nervous system.

"The hot blush on the cheek of modesty, the ashen pallor on the face of fear, the beads of perspiration upon the brow of responsibility, and the parched breath upon the lip of embarrassment are but passing shadows of the fitful play of vaso-motor innervation."

The most serious, and, therefore, the most important disturbances of function in neurasthenia are disorders of digestion.

If the appetite, digestion and power of assimilation are disturbed, the patient may become greatly reduced in health because the tissues of the body cannot then be sufficiently nourished.

This condition is very common and by far the greatest number of dyspepsias are of the nervous variety.

The stomach neuroses may be manifested in the form of severe pain, paroxysmal in character, and forming the so-called gastric crises; or there may be secretory changes causing subacidity or hyperacidity with complaint of pressure, distention and eructations, and feelings of malaise, headache and dizziness; or the symptoms may be those of peristaltic unrest, in which there is vomiting, regurgitation or rumination.

Other digestive disorders, such as constipation and attacks of diarrhœa, are frequent in neurotic persons.

Disturbance of the sexual function is perhaps the most frequent of all disorders that occur with the neurotic diathesis.

A very grave perversion of sexual desire belongs rather to the category of insanity, in which a marked exaggeration of the sexual promptings is known as satyriasis, or nymphomania, when it occurs in women.

In men the symptoms are those of impotence, premature ejaculation, sense of prostration after sexual intercourse, etc.

With persons of a nervous tendency, both male and female, slight irritations of the genital tract produce very serious results. They cause the subjects to be filled with fear and dread, and their mental conditon is most pitiable.

Pelvic disorders, even when painless, may act as foci of morbid excitation, and very often operations are sought by these patients and undertaken by the surgeon more for the effect of creating a starting point of new hope and encouragement than for removing the abnormal condition, which is often but very slight.

With such a procedure the powerful factor with some patients is the feeling that now, at last, the real cause of the ailment has been found, and this factor can be counted on the most in cases where many other treatments have been tried in vain.

There is in some of the neurasthenics a disturbance of metabolism which may seem to be at fault, and where it is impossible to say whether or not the nervous disorder is the primary cause of the condition.

In these instances of lithæmia, or gouty diathesis,

the urine is abnormal and often contains uric acid, urates, oxalates and phosphates.

When the condition is traceable to diseases of the liver, gouty heredity, or to absorption of the products of faulty digestion, the nervous symptoms may be considered secondary; but there is little or no doubt that the nervous weakness may be the primary affection, and even in many cases of gouty parentage, it is probable that the impaired nervous system is often a direct inheritant. (Putnam.)

There are two general types of neurotic persons.

In one there is an element of feebleness, both physical and mental, which is the prominent feature, though the patient may be over-fat and be at the same time anæmic.

Owing to the excitability and misdirected force, the nervousness is shown by the exaggerated response to slight irritation.

The other type is what has been called the intellectual. These are usually slight, spare and active, with sharp, prominent features and hollow cheeks and temples. The limbs are small but often sinewy, and the absence of fat in the muscles gives the quality of hardness under the hand. The pulse becomes accelerated upon the least excitement, with color painted high upon the cheeks, if the complexion be not sallow. The conversation is lively and voluble and many times brilliant and keen. In society they are gay, full of spirit and often fascinating, but at home they are mostly depressed, fretful and "fidgety." They have frequent attacks of headache, windy colic and stomach ache.

They suffer from neuralgias, which are many times uterine or ovarian.

The difference between the hysterical and the neurotic woman is described by Dr. Allbutt as follows: "The neurotic woman is sensitive, zealous, managing, self-forgetful, wearing herself for others; the hysteric, whether languid or impulsive, is purposeless, introspective, and selfish. In one is the defect of endurance, but in the other, defect of higher gifts and dominion of mind."

It may be gathered from the foregoing rather lengthy description of what is understood by nervousness, that almost any discomfort or ailment may be experienced by people who are neurotic, without there being any appreciable bodily lesion.

To them their sufferings appear real enough but to another a sufficient cause, or one that would produce a like result in an organism that was working harmoniously, does not become apparent.

The relation of this state to organic disease is obscure, but none the less important.

It is so often associated with disordered metabolism and nutrition that many organs or tissues may lose their vitality.

The frequent disturbance of the heart and vasomotor system leads to the rational inference that the nervous derangement must occasionally pave the way or mark the beginning of some serious organic affection.

Mother nature does not herself destroy and does not save. She simply evolves, and if she were conscious she would not be indifferent. Stand in her way and she hurts; act in harmony with her and she improves. With her sunshine she brings growth, warmth and sunstrokes; her moonlight encourages lovers and favors depredations; her rain quenches man's thirst and drowns him; her wind purifies and favors fertilization and makes cyclones. She has no predilection and no reasoning, but is simply cause and effect. She can be guided by the logical mind or misguided by whim and sentiment. Her necessities are engaged in a continuous strife for supremacy, and in matters of life and health it is by utilizing or combating her doings that man is cared for and cured, and it makes no difference to nature whether we protest or comply—the result is always the same.

The most exacting epochs in a woman's career, or when she is prone to become nervous and have functional disturbances, are the times of puberty, marriage and the change of life.

During these times there are the most abrupt alterations in the functions of her genitalia and her nervous system must become accustomed to the changes in her pelvic organs.

Other critical times are the periods of menstruation and pregnancy.

It is very probable that primitive women had no menstrual disorders, and even at the present time some of the uncivilized women have but slight troubles with child-bearing.

The different situations of life make a vast difference in the ability to maintain composure. Circumstances have different effects upon women in very much the same way as climate has upon vegetation.

Some fruits and cereals are more hardy than others, as they thrive better and require different climatic conditions.

There is a vast difference in the nervous state when the sexes mingle freely and when they are separated.

The requirements of the intimacy of marriage cannot be compared to the natural exactions of a life of seclusion. In one there is the constant liability to excitement from extrinsic causes, while the other has only the intrinsic promptings to control.

There is no one who is so stable as not to become excited or depressed, and the pendulum more or less regularly oscillates between the one and the other to maintain a balance. If it be drawn markedly in one direction it reacts only with greater force in the opposite before an equilibrium is established.

The functions of animal life are performed by means of sympathetic, or reflex, action, in which the different organs act in concert or co-ordination.

Congestion alone excites to reflex action, and when this becomes pronounced or exaggerated the condition is one of nervousness.

Because of the abundant blood supply to the pelvic organs and the equally liberal nerve supply, their congested condition causes great reflex activity. With distension of the erectile tissue, or physiological congestion, there is excitement.

Reflex phenomena may be manifested by the modification of the quantity or quality of some secretion, or by the production of spasmodic contractions in either voluntary or involuntary muscles.

Both the centripetal and the centrifugal nerves

which cause the reflex action of digestion are of the sympathetic system. The same nervous mechanism is concerned in uniting the various generative functions and in many pathological phenomena.

When the center through which these nerves pass is in a state of exalted activity, the mind has less control than usual, and abnormalities of secretion and spasmodic contractions occur with slight irritation.

In case the centripetal nerve involved in the reflex action is of the sympathetic system and the other of the cerebro-spinal, the result is a convulsion.

Occasionally cerebral excitation or mental emotions may take the place of peripheric impressions and incite abnormal reflex actions.

A nervous condition may be said to be one in which there is a susceptibility to abnormal reflex action.

Spasmodic conditions cannot be found post-mortem and hence an adequate physical abnormality cannot readily be demonstrated in cases of neurasthenia.

Very slight lesions, irritations, congestions or impressions may cause spasms or alterated secretion when the nervous system is below the ordinary standard and wanting in stability, and thus we find very different effects of physical changes in different women.

Some women bear marked uterine displacements or gross lesions of the genitalia with comparatively little discomfort, while many suffer greatly with but slight circulatory changes in the generative organs.

It is generally conceded that the genital organs are responsible for much nervous excitability, and the condition may be due to the great liability to reflex action from this source.

The spirit of unrest that pervades throughout our American cities is evidence of increasing nervousness.

One has but to observe the large and constantly increasing number of people who are wearing glasses in order to relieve the strain put upon their nervous systems by defective vision, to be convinced of the extent of weakness. There is no good reason why eyes should be less perfect than ears, heads, limbs or other organs of the body, but the delicate nervous mechanism of sight makes disturbance and reflex actions quite common when the nervous system is not equal to any strain.

Many ailments are, in the opinion of some oculists, attributed to eye strain. Dr. Stevens says: "Nearly all headaches, neuralgias, almost all cases of chorea and fifty per cent. of all cases of epilepsy, are due to inco-ordination of the muscles of the eyeball."

This is a very broad statement and cannot, of course, be proven, though everyone recognizes the fact that errors of refraction may cause headaches.

Some of the so-called "remote effects of eye strain" are so very remote that it is very difficult to connect the cause with the effect, for with a reasonably stable center it would require an extraordinary defect in the apparatus of vision to produce abnormal reflex actions in the abdomen.

The delicate mechanism of the eye is one of the first portions of the nervous apparatus to be disturbed by any undue strain upon the system, but if we inquire into the results obtained by the most cautious and experienced oculists, it grows evident that many effects attributed to eye strain have much wider causes. Power, of England, has investigated the relations of the sexual system to eye disease and points out that many serious complaints of the eye are caused by abnormal sexual relations and by disorders of menstruation, and the frequent association of difficult vision with sexual disorders would indicate that eye troubles were rather a secondary than a primal cause of many of the symptoms of defective innervation.

Diseases of the stomach are either primary or secondary—mostly secondary.

Digestion depends chiefly upon the integrity of the the nerve supply, and dyspepsia is only a symptom and becomes manifest with an abnormality of any vital organ.

The stomach acts in sympathy with every constitutional alteration, and inasmuch as digestion and assimilation are brought about only by normal reflex action, any disturbance in the equilibrium of the sympathetic nervous system must have its effect upon the digestive apparatus.

Practically, there are but two primary diseases of the stomach—cancer and ulcer—and when there is a disturbance of appetite and digestion there will, except in these two instances, be an affection of some other part of the digestive tract or vital organ with which the stomach acts in sympathy.

The effect of mental emotions upon digestion may be observed daily. When the patient is unduly sensitive there is a corresponding liability to digestive disturbances.

A suitable moral and social, as well as physical, environment is essential for normal digestive activity.

Probably the most frequent of all abnormal reflex actions are the alterations in intestinal peristalsis, a diminishing of which causes constipation and an exaggeration producing diarrhœa.

Chomel wrote: "A person digests as much with his legs as with his stomach."

It is not alone the person's locomotion that has this effect, but the mental machinery and the sexual apparatus also influence the digestive function.

Exercise promotes the appetite, increases the bodily waste and needs, facilitates nutrition, and, under proper conditions, is an aid to digestion. The daily farm laborer awaits impatiently his meal time and eats all the more on account of his hard work; but if his fatigue is too great, his appetite is lost.

The same obtains in mental activity. This is known and conceded by all observers.

In their work on Diseases of the Stomach, Van Valsah and Nisbet thus refer to the dynamic affections of this organ:

"All the disorders of the stomach which present no characteristic pathological anatomy are classified as dynamic affections. * * * Practically, this is one of the most important sections of the pathology of the stomach. Here disease presents itself in its genesis, and the subsequent evolution, unless arrested by proper treatment, may be represented by an inverted pyramid. The trouble grows along deviating lines, and becomes more and more irresistible. The physiological functions, one after the other, are enlisted with the forces which make for disease. The disease should be recognized and crushed in its pre-anatomical stage if permanent damage is to be avoided. This is the period when treatment will show its greatest power and give the most brilliant re. sults. * * * These peculiarities are often due to the existence of a trouble in some other part of the body which selects the stomach as the center of its manifestation. The dynamic affections of the stomach develop preferably in a particular soil. This is the neurotic or nervous temperament or constitution. Some persons are born with a delicate and overwrought nervous system, and others acquire it by the mode of life, by bad habits, and by too exclusive and excessive mental or moral developments. The resulting condition is unstable nervous equilibrium—the forerunner often of the nervous affections of the stomach. Most of these affections are more frequent in women than in men, the proportion being about one to ten in youth, and gradually changing until the sexual difference becomes much less (about one to two) during the last third of life. The chief exciting causes in men are mental overwork and the reverses of fortune. The dynamic affections are common among women near the end of the social season in large cities, and are less frequent among country girls; for in spite of the pure air and sunshine of the country and the freedom from the withering touch of culture,' anxiety and sorrow and disappointment, and disorders of menstruation, of reproduction, and lactation, have the same influence in the hut as in the palace. The predominance in women may be explained in part by their mode of life, their delicate organization, and their peculiar diseases."

Worry, or a state of disturbance from care and anxiety, is a very frequent cause of digestive disturbance. Dunin remarked that "it is too often supposed that hypochondriasis and other neuroses are caused by constipation when the reverse is true, and constipation is caused by them."

When digestion is disturbed there is faulty nutrition, and when any organs are deprived of proper nutrition these organs cannot perform their functions in a normal manner.

We have then to consider the primal cause of unnecessary worry, which is perhaps the first indication of a nervous condition.

In the lower animal life the female is quite as stable, hardy and vigorous as the male, and among the more uncivilized people women are hardly less frail and weakly than men.

In these modern times the female sex has become known as being the weaker, and almost any observer will have noticed that the proportion of nervous individuals is very much larger among females, and that nervous women greatly outnumber men who have neurotic ailments.

The same physical laws apply to both sexes alike, and in a given community the same food, water, air and general conditions under which the two sexes live are identical.

The hereditary influences are likewise similar and the essential environments practically the same. There must be an underlying cause for this variation in nervous stability which we must look for in the differential organs, and we are forced to attribute at least a considerable share of the trouble to the influence of the sexual life.

Probably the greater proportion of nervous men are to be classed as sexual neurasthenics, but we are not in the habit of referring to women as such.

If irritable weakness of the male sexual organs causes neurasthenia, the constitutional effects from the disturbance of the female genitalia ought certainly, by reason of the more intimate connection, be a greater cause of a nervous condition.

Every patholigical, and often a physiological, condition of the female sexual apparatus is accompanied by nervous symptoms. No grave uterine trouble affects the system for any length of time without reacting to some extent upon the general health. The nervous system becomes greatly disordered, the functions under its influence are badly performed, and derangement of the blood is the invariable result. (Munde).

Osler maintains that neuroses of the stomach occur chiefly in women with menstrual disturbances and hysteria.

We believe with Thomas that in the order of their frequency and importance the following primary pathological conditions must be considered to constitute the special factors of uterine disease:

1st—Catarrhal condition of the lining membrane.

2nd—Prolonged congestion of uterine tissues

3rd—Excessive growth of connective or muscular tissues.

The first condition may be found in the virgin, in the childless married woman, and in the woman who has borne children.

The second condition follows more or less closely upon the first, depends upon similar causes, and is intimately connected with them.

The third condition is merely the last link in the chain, and the natural consequences of a long continuance of the first two.

Whatever tends to produce and maintain any of these primary conditions is likely to establish confirmed uterine disease.

That a very large proportion, if not the majority, of modern women have some disturbance which may be reasonably attributed to the condition of their pelvic organs is highly probable.

In cases of nervousness in either sex it may be found that, as a rule, the first indication is a disturbance of the sexual function, following which there will be digestive troubles, and then affections of special nerves, of which disorders of sight are the first and most frequent, with neuralgias, etc., later.

Observation has shown this to be the general rule, and that is also in accordance with the law of self-preservation.

With the conviction that nervousness is first manifested and begins with an alteration in the natural sexual function, we may conclude that other functional disorders are a natural sequence.

It thus becomes evident that the most prolific cause of nervousness is an inability for natural sexual living.

Having ascertained the cause of an ailment, it is the physician's duty to exert himself and put forth every effort within his power to remove that cause, for in no other manner can a cure be hoped for or the patient's condition greatly improved.

The utmost that medicine can do is to act as a spur to nature.

Only by stimulating to functional activity, or by relieving excitement to over-activity, can abnormalities be restored and a normal condition maintained.

Nervous patients are sensitive and easily wounded. The mind is particularly sensitive to the dark colors and the brightness of life is decreased, while its gloom is magnified.

Monotony is unfavorable to life, and for those whose functions are depressed and to whom the world looks gloomy, there must needs be something to stir up animation, and the emotional waves of sexual activity serve this purpose because they "lash into movement the dreary calm of the sea's soul" and produce a welcome alternation.

The advice of the greatest of religious reformers was sound and good, when, in alluding to young women who were nervous and had dreams, he advised such in his "Table Talk" to be married at once, thereby "taking the medicine that God has given."

It has been said with truth, that neurasthenic patients are cured, not by physic, but by the physician.

The treatment as usually outlined consists in giving such drugs as will improve the vigor of the nervous system; the use of baths, electricity, and massage, the "rest cure," or a change of scene and climate, and the improvement of nutrition by social and moral measures.

Uterine disorders and eye diseases are corrected,

and not infrequently ovariotomy and other surgical measures have been resorted to.

Success is variable and depends upon the impression made upon the mind of the patient.

Nervousness invariably results from conditions that interfere with the natural functions.

A certain amount of sexual excitement is physiological, for which nature has provided but one wholly adequate method of relief.

When the organism does not respond to the usual stimulation to functional activity, but reacts irregularly, there is a state of nervous instability.

The condition is one of tension or spasm in some part of the body, which prevents the organs from acting co-ordinately, and hence one function is unduly excited or exaggerated and another depressed.

The sexual function, as previously stated, is usually the first one to be disturbed, and when this irregularity has been corrected, the abnormality will generally have been overcome.

We are called upon to consider the patients as we find them, and having determined the existing condition, render such aid as will be effective.

The first indication is a removal of the cause, and this is always advised, but the great problem that confronts us and which demands solution, is how to accomplish this in practice.

Whether the cause be recognized by the patient and the laity or not, should make no difference to the physician, and if a cure is to be obtained it can only be brought about by the establishment of the normal bodily functions.

The one object in view is to restore a proper sympathetic, or reflex, action.

During waking hours there is always some little muscular or other tension, and when this becomes emphasized and amounts to a more or less spasmodic condition there is excitability, restlessness or nervousness. Sleep does not occur without relaxation.

Tension or congestion of the generative apparatus produces sexual excitement, and the circulation is equalized and the whole system relaxed by the involuntary orgasm, which is the physiological method of restoring equilibrium and relaxation.

What a certain class of surgeons claim to accomplish in their efforts to cure chronic ailments by forcibly dilating sphincter muscles, is done by nature during the involuntary actions attending a venereal crisis.

The constitutional effect upon the vaso-motor nervous system by an orgasm is all that is claimed by these "orificial surgeons" for their method, and much more may be accomplished in the treatment of chronic nervous disorders by the natural, than by artificial means.

Where there is a local physical condition sufficient to cause abnormal frequency of excitement it should be removed, but the vast majority of women suffer by reason of depression of their sexual function and want of natural gratification.

There is nothing that will give such life to both men and women and make them feel and remain young, as the conviction of their own virility and sexual activity; nor is there anything to compare with the salutary effects of reasonable sexual exercise.

The rejuvenating influence of conscious possession of an ability for the expression of love is not recognized by women.

Among men it is well known and taken advantage of by irregular practitioners for the purpose of parting depressed men from their money, but the condition of women is not usually viewed in such a light.

When the ordinary man is under any strain or begins to worry, the first manifestation is a depression of his sexual function, and straightway he is prompted to seek aid.

Such depression leads to digestive or other functional disorders, which are only relieved by his conviction of returning vigor.

Very often something more than advice is required to convince him that he is sufficiently potent, and hence the multiplicity of remedies for impotency.

With the average female the course is somewhat different.

The same rule applies to both and the same conditions obtain, but she is not apt to notice a similar functional depression, or physical deficiency, and is guided only by her feelings.

The importunities of the husband with whom she must live become irksome and disgusting because she does not respond to his advances, but it never occurs to her that her discomfort is the result of her own physical state.

Every time she yields without desire her condition is aggravated, as she is only irritated and not relieved by the embrace.

She will readily notice her depression of spirits

and will be quick to detect any change in her complexion or facial expression.

Her unsatisfactory position makes her unable to withstand the ravages of time, and she is alarmed by her fading bloom and fleeting gracefulness.

She may seek to improve or preserve her bodily contour by whatever means are suggested, and attention is often given to the bust and great efforts put forth for cosmetic purposes.

The medicines recommended and taken by nervous women are the same as those used by deficient men.

Strychnia, phosphorus and other nerve tonics are given to both alike, and almost every other measure is resorted to instead of the most effective means to maintain and restore personal and family comfort, health and attractiveness.

The woman's marital relations are already strained, and, unlike the man, who eagerly invites and anxiously looks for physical evidence of vigor, she resists, despises and disdains to avail herself of nature's "fountain of youth."

Too much stress is being laid upon the exactions of social functions and their debilitating effects upon society women.

It is true that social duties are wearing, but most of the evening affairs of society are attended by men as well, for society ladies require the escort of their husbands when they attend affairs for amusement.

During the day these men are usually subjected to the cares of business, which are generally greater than the self-imposed household duties of the wife, who, it will often be found, enjoys a longer period of repose.

A wife can only be removed from the influences that excite the sexual passion by separation from her husband and the ordinary society.

This is wholly impractical and should not be considered, and so long as she lives under the existing conditions she must have the relief from the excitement occasioned by her surroundings and be in a physical condition that permits of her availing herself of nature's requirement.

When the sexual organs are sufficiently vigorous to meet the exactions of the system there will not only be personal bodily harmony, but the woman's actions will be in keeping with her surroundings and she will be enabled to live in unison and rythm with her family and society.

The mental condition must inevitably follow the physical state, and since the sexual function is the first to be depressed, a reaction is most effectively produced by attention to the generative organs.

In this way the nervous condition is overcome by natural means, which is the only rational method of relief. It is not necessary for the physician to tell the woman of her sexual debility and, moreover, it would be difficult to convince her that therein lies the chief cause of her troubles, but nervousness is simply lack of harmony, which must be restored if there is to be healthful and, therefore, happy living.

In the treatment of nervous women the author has seen most happy results follow local applications to the genital organs.

By the use of preparations of nux vomica, Cannabis Indica, resorcin, glycerine and a chlorinated compound of alcohol, a reaction to nervous depression may be obtained, a cheerful frame of mind established and the woman put in a way for natural living.

Whenever a wife is conscious of the promptings of her womanly nature, the coming of the husband is anxiously looked for, and he is met with an inviting smile and greeted affectionately. His presence inspires animation, and the hopeful, cheering mien of the wife becomes contagious, and the hearthstone is brightened and the home transformed into a peaceful abiding place.

The physical condition causes the mind to be filled with thoughts of him who is known to bring the greatest of pleasurable feelings, followed by contented rest. The joyful anticipations beget a desire to please, and innumerable little acts that are known to be appreciated are contemplated and executed, as there is then a very natural "desiring of desire."

With a congenial mate who is impelled to cheerful compliance with the innermost longings, that man must be wholly depraved who is not attracted and does not hasten to the side of her whose presence thrills and whose touch alleviates.

The irresistible desire to fly to the peaceful refuge afforded by the outstretched arms of a loving woman is well known, and history teems with tales of those who have risked their all by reason of this allurement,

The modern detective takes advantage of the force of this unerring inclination and seeks out and watches the criminal's loved one, knowing that he is most apt to find the fugitive where his masculinity is attracted with the greatest force.

The dominating influence in drawing men is recognized by non-medical writers and given by Howard in these words: "The animating impulse of all organic life is the sexual instinct. It is that which underlies the struggle for existence in the animal world, and is the source of all human endeavor and emotion. That affinity that draws the two sexes together for the production of a new being, that overmastering, unanswered impulse, is the most powerful which pertains to the human family, and has ever been the cause and subject of man's most exalted thought. There is an intimate and unavoidable relationship existing between the mind and the sexual instinct, and were man deprived of this instinct, all ambition, affection and endeavor, all poetry, art and religion, in fact all emotions and achievements inspired by what we term love, would cease, and the world would become cold and passionless, destitute of sentiment or aspiration, devoid of any incentive to progress or energy, while the intimate and reciprocal machinery of human society, robbed of its motive force, would come to a stop and crumble away in hopeless disorganization."

The intimate association of the sweetest and noblest with the most carnal human emotions, was observed by Marion Crawford, who wisely states:

"There can be passion without love—there can be no love without passion."

It is in the family that love is to be developed and nourished.

In this material world of ours love cannot long abide where there is no manifestation of the sexual passion.

To retain the love of a normal husband in the prime of life, the wife should possess such qualifications as will supply his requirements.

Perhaps the greatest source of sin and misery in domestic life is to be traced to unsatisfactory sexual conditions.

A careful study of the cases of domestic infelicity will reveal the fact that the discord arises from unequalized sexuality.

It may also be found that most often the wife is the one with whom the deficiency lies.

The most effective way to deal practically with these undesirable states is to render such aid as will most speedily and easily supply such deficiency.

The glory and strength of radiant womanhood must be restored from within, and then there will be not only personal harmony but family unity.

Women with sexual apathy, either comparative or absolute, are the most jealous and exacting of wives, and experience has proven that nervous, irritable, cross, fault-finding and dissatisfied wives are transformed into buoyant, cheerful, amiable, contented and companionable helpmeets by proper treatment directed to the cause of the trouble—the sexual organs.

This sternly practical age has made the days more prosaic and lessened the amount of true sentiment and romance; but healthy, active, differential organs will ever cause hearts to grow fond and manners gentle.

Civilization has refined and educated, but the primal instinct is still the same, and there will always be marriage and giving in marriage.

When people live closer to nature they will be less nervous.

With the celestial fire kindled in the hearts of both wife and husband, the whole family circle will be illumined—and this can occur only with the actions of a proper SEXUAL LIFE.

INDEX